PHILOSOPHY

FROM **PLATO AND SOCRATES** TO
ETHICS AND METAPHYSICS,
AN ESSENTIAL PRIMER ON
THE **HISTORY OF THOUGHT**

101

PAUL KLEINMAN

Avon, Massachusetts

Published by
Adams Media, a division of F+W Media, Inc.
57 Littlefield Street, Avon, MA 02322. U.S.A.
www.adamsmedia.com

ISBN 10: 1-4405-6767-0
ISBN 13: 978-1-4405-6767-4
eISBN 10: 1-4405-6768-9
eISBN 13: 978-1-4405-6768-1

Printed in the United States of America.

10   9   8   7   6

Cover images © Jupiterimages Corporation and 123rf.com.
Interior illustrations by Eric Andrews.

*This book is available at quantity discounts for bulk purchases.
For information, please call 1-800-289-0963.*

CONTENTS

INTRODUCTION

What Is Philosophy?

The very question sounds philosophical, doesn't it? But what exactly does that mean? What *is* philosophy?

The word *philosophy* means "love of wisdom." Indeed, it is a love of wisdom that guides philosophers to explore the fundamental questions about who we are and why we're here. On the surface, philosophy is a social science. But as you read this book, you'll discover that it is so much more than that. Philosophy touches on every subject you could possibly think of. It's not just a bunch of old Greek guys asking each other questions over and over again (though it has its fair share of that as well). Philosophy has very real applications; from the ethical questions raised in government policy to the logic forms required in computer programming, everything has its roots in philosophy.

Through philosophy, we are able to explore concepts like the meaning of life, knowledge, morality, reality, the existence of God, consciousness, politics, religion, economics, art, linguistics—philosophy has no bounds!

In a very broad sense, there are six major themes philosophy touches on:

1. **Metaphysics:** The study of the universe and reality
2. **Logic:** How to create a valid argument

3. **Epistemology:** The study of knowledge and how we acquire knowledge
4. **Aesthetics:** The study of art and beauty
5. **Politics:** The study of political rights, government, and the role of citizens
6. **Ethics:** The study of morality and how one should live his life

If you've ever thought, "Oh, *philosophy*. I'll never be able to understand *that* stuff," then fear not. This is the crash course in philosophy that you've always wanted. Finally, you'll be able to open your mind without making your eyes bleed.

Welcome to Philosophy 101.

PRE-SOCRATIC

The origins of Western philosophy

The roots of Western philosophy can be found in the work of Greek philosophers during the fifth and sixth centuries. These philosophers, later referred to as pre-Socratic, started to question the world around them. Rather than attributing their surroundings to the Greek gods, these philosophers searched for more rational explanations that could explain the world, the universe, and their existence.

This was a philosophy of nature. Pre-Socratic philosophers questioned where everything came from, what everything was created from, how nature could be described mathematically, and how one could explain the existence of plurality in nature. They sought to find a primary principle, known as *archê*, which was the basic material of the universe. Due to the fact that not everything in the universe looks the same or remains in the same exact state, pre-Socratic philosophers determined that there must be principles of change that the *archê* contained.

WHAT DOES *PRE-SOCRATIC* MEAN?

The term *pre-Socratic*, meaning "before Socrates," was popularized in 1903 by German scholar Hermann Diels. Socrates was actually alive during the same time as many of the pre-Socratic philosophers, and therefore the term does not imply that these philosophies existed prior to those of Socrates. Rather, the term *pre-Socratic* relates to the difference in ideology and principles. While many pre-Socratic philosophers produced texts, none have fully survived and most of what we understand about the pre-Socratic philosophers is based on the fragments of text that remain and the quotes of later historians and philosophers, which were usually biased.

IMPORTANT PRE-SOCRATIC SCHOOLS

The Milesian School

The first pre-Socratic philosophers existed in the city of Miletus, along the western coast of Anatolia (modern Turkey). From Miletus came three important pre-Socratic philosophers: Thales, Anaximander, and Anaximenes.

Thales

One of the most important pre-Socratic philosophers, Thales (624–546 B.C.), claimed the *archê*, or the single element, was water. Thales determined that water could experience principles of change like evaporation and condensation, therefore allowing for it to be gaseous or solid. He also knew that water was responsible for moisture (which heat was generated from) and nourishment. Thales even believed the earth floated on water.

Anaximander

Following Thales, the next major philosopher to come out of Miletus was Anaximander (610–546 B.C.). Unlike Thales, Anaximander claimed the single element was actually an undefined, unlimited, and indefinite substance, known as *apeiron*. From this, opposites like moist and dry and cold and hot separated from each other. Anaximander is known for being the first philosopher that we know of to have left writings of his work.

Anaximenes
The last important pre-Socratic philosopher of the Milesian school was Anaximenes (585–528 B.C.), who believed the single element was air. According to Anaximenes, air is everywhere and has the ability to undergo processes and become transformed into other things, such as water, clouds, wind, fire, and even the earth.

The Pythagorean School
Philosopher and mathematician Pythagoras (570–497 B.C.), perhaps most famous for the Pythagorean theorem named after him, believed that the basis of all reality was mathematical relations and that mathematics governed everything. To Pythagoras, numbers were sacred, and with the use of mathematics, everything could be measured and predicted. The impact and image of Pythagoras was astounding. His school was cult-like, with followers listening to his every word . . . and even his strange rules, which covered anything from what and what not to eat, how to dress, and even how to urinate. Pythagoras philosophized on many areas, and his students believed that his teachings were the prophecies of the gods.

The Ephesian School
The Ephesian school was based on the work of one man, Heraclitus of Ephesus (535–475 B.C.). Heraclitus believed that everything in nature is constantly changing, or in a state of flux. He is perhaps most famous for his notion that one cannot step in the same river twice. Heraclitus believed that the single element was fire and that everything was a manifestation of fire.

The Eleatic School

The Eleatic school was based in Colophon, an ancient city not far from Miletus. From this region came four important pre-Socratic philosophers: Xenophanes, Parmenides, Zeno, and Melissus.

Xenophanes of Colophon

Xenophanes (570–475 B.C.) is known for his critique of religion and mythology. In particular, he attacked the notion that the gods were anthropomorphic (or took a human form). Xenophanes believed there was one god that, while it did not physically move, had the ability to hear, see, and think, and controlled the world with his thoughts.

Parmenides of Elea

Parmenides (510–440 B.C.) believed reality didn't have to do with the world one experienced and that it was only through reason, not the senses, that one would be able to arrive at the truth. Parmenides concluded that the work of earlier Milesian philosophers was not only unintelligible; they were asking the wrong questions to begin with. To Parmenides, it made no sense to discuss what is and what is not, for the only intelligible thing to discuss, and the only thing that is true, is what is (what exists).

Parmenides had an incredible impact on Plato and all of Western philosophy. His work led the school of Elea to become the first movement to use pure reason as the only criterion for finding truth.

Zeno of Elea

Zeno of Elea (490–430 B.C.) was Parmenides' most famous student (and possibly his lover), who devoted his time to creating arguments (known as paradoxes) that defended Parmenides' ideas.

In Zeno's most famous paradoxes, the paradoxes of motion, he attempted to show that ontological pluralism, the notion that many things exist as opposed to one, will actually lead to conclusions that are absurd. Parmenides and Zeno believed that reality existed as one thing, and that things like plurality and motion were nothing more than illusions. Though the work of Zeno would later be disproved, his paradoxes still raise important questions, challenges, and inspirations for philosophers, physicists, and mathematicians.

Melissus of Samos

Melissus of Samos, who lived around 440 B.C., was the last philosopher of the Eleatic school. Continuing the ideas of Parmenides and Zeno of Elea, Melissus of Samos distinguished between *is* and *seems*. When a thing *is* X, according to Melissus of Samos, it has to always be X (and never not X). Therefore, according to this idea, when something is cold, it can never stop being cold. But since this is not the case, and properties are not retained indefinitely, nothing (except for the Parmenidean Real, reality existing as one continuous, unchanging thing) actually ever *is*; rather, it *seems*.

The Atomist School

The Atomist school, started by Leucippus in the fifth century B.C. and passed down by his student, Democritus (460–370 B.C.), believed that every physical object is made up of atoms and void (empty space that atoms move in) that are arranged in different ways. This idea is not too far from the concepts of atoms that we know today. This school believed that atoms were incredibly small particles (so small that they could not be cut in half) that differed in size, shape, motion, arrangement, and position, and that when put together, these atoms created what is seen in the visible world.

SOCRATES (469–399 B.C.)

The game-changer

Socrates was born in Athens, Greece, around 469 B.C. and died in 399 B.C. Whereas pre-Socratic philosophers examined the natural world, Socrates placed emphasis on the human experience. He focused on individual morality, questioned what made a good life, and discussed social and political questions. His work and his ideas became the foundation of Western philosophy. While Socrates is widely regarded as one of the wisest men to have ever lived, he never wrote down any of his thoughts, and all that we know about him is based on the written works of his students and contemporaries (mainly the works of Plato, Xenophon, and Aristophanes).

Because everything that we know about Socrates is based on accounts from others (which were often fictionalized) and these accounts differ, we do not actually know much about him or his teachings. This is known as the "Socratic problem." From the texts of others, we are able to gather that he was the son of a stone mason and a midwife; he most likely had a basic Greek education; he was not aesthetically good-looking (during a time when external beauty was very important); he served in the military during the Peloponnesian War; he had three sons with a much younger woman; and he lived in poverty. He might have worked as a stone mason before turning to philosophy.

The one detail that has been well documented, however, is Socrates' death. While Socrates was alive, the state of Athens began to decline. Having embarrassingly lost to Sparta in the Peloponnesian War, Athens had an identity crisis of sorts and became fixated on physical beauty, ideas of wealth, and romanticizing the past. Because

Socrates was an outspoken critic of this way of life, he grew to have many enemies. In 399 B.C., Socrates was arrested and brought to trial with charges of being unreligious and corrupting the city's youth. Socrates was found guilty and was sentenced to death by poisonous drink. Rather than flee into exile (which he had the chance to do), Socrates drank the poison without any hesitation.

SOCRATES' CONTRIBUTION TO PHILOSOPHY

A quote often attributed to Socrates is, "The unexamined life is not worth living." Socrates believed that in order for a person to be wise, that individual must be able to understand himself. To Socrates, an individual's actions were directly related to his intelligence and ignorance. He believed people should develop their self, rather than concentrate on material objects, and he sought to understand the difference between *acting* good and *being* good. It was in the new and unique way that he approached knowledge, consciousness, and morality that Socrates would forever change philosophy.

The Socratic Method

Socrates is perhaps most famous for his Socratic method. First described in Plato's *Socratic Dialogues*, Socrates and a pupil would have a discussion on a particular issue, and through a series of questions, Socrates would set out to discover the driving force behind how that individual's beliefs and sentiments were shaped and in so doing, get closer to the truth. By continually asking questions, Socrates was able to expose contradictions in the way an individual thought, which allowed him to come to a solid conclusion.

Socrates used the elenchus, a method in which he would refute the claims of the other person. Here are the steps of the elenchus:

1. An individual would assert a statement to Socrates, which Socrates would then refute. Or, Socrates might ask the other person a question, such as, "What is courage?"

2. Once the other person provides his answer, Socrates would think of a scenario where his answer was not the case, asking him to assume his original statement was false. For example, if the other person describes courage as "endurance of the soul," Socrates might refute this claim by saying that "Courage is a fine thing," while "Ignorant endurance is not a fine thing."

3. The other person would agree with this claim, and Socrates would then change the statement to include the exception to the rule.

4. Socrates proves that the individual's statement is false and that the negation is in fact true. As the other person continues to alter his answer, Socrates continues refuting, and through this, the individual's answer gets closer to the actual truth.

The Socratic Method Today

The Socratic method is still widely used to this day, most notably in law schools throughout the United States. First, a student will be asked to summarize a judge's argument. Then, the student will be asked if he agrees with the judge's argument. The professor will then act as devil's advocate by asking a series of questions to make the student defend his decision.

By using the Socratic method, students are able to start thinking critically and using logic and reasoning to create their arguments, while also finding and patching up holes in their positions.

PLATO (429–347 B.C.)

One of the founders of Western philosophy

Plato was born in Athens, Greece, around 429 B.C. to parents who were members of the Greek aristocracy. Because of his social class, Plato was taught by many distinguished educators. However, no individual would have as great an impact on him as Socrates and his ability to debate and create a dialogue. In fact, the written works of Plato are where much of the information we know about Socrates comes from.

While he was expected by his family to pursue a career in politics, two events would lead Plato away from this lifestyle: the Peloponnesian War (in which, upon Sparta's victory, several of Plato's relatives were part of a dictatorship, but were removed for being corrupt) and the execution of Socrates in 399 B.C. by the new Athenian government.

Plato then turned toward philosophy and began writing and traveling. He studied under Pythagoras in Sicily and, upon returning to Athens, founded the Academy, a school where he and other likeminded individuals taught and discussed philosophy and mathematics. Among Plato's students was Aristotle.

PLATO'S PHILOSOPHY THROUGH WRITTEN CONVERSATIONS

Like Socrates, Plato believed philosophy was a process of continuous questioning and dialogues, and his writing appeared in this format.

Two of the most interesting things about these dialogues are that Plato's own opinions on the subject matters he wrote about were never explicitly stated (though with in-depth research, one might be able to infer his stance) and that he was never a character in his writing. Plato wanted readers to have the ability to form their own opinions on the subjects and not be told how to think (this also proves how skillful a writer he was). For this reason, many of his dialogues do not reach a concise conclusion. Those that do, however, allow for possible counterarguments and doubts.

Plato's dialogues dealt with a variety of subject matters, including things such as art, theater, ethics, immortality, the mind, and metaphysics.

There are at least thirty-six dialogues written by Plato, as well as thirteen letters (though historians dispute the letters' authenticity).

THE THEORY OF FORMS

One of the most important concepts Plato developed was his theory of Forms. Plato states that reality exists on two specific levels:

1. The visible world that is made up of sights and sounds
2. The intelligible world (the world of Forms) that gives the visible world its being

For example, when a person sees a beautiful painting, that person has the ability to identify beauty because he has an abstract concept of what beauty is. Therefore, beautiful things are seen as beautiful because they are a part of the Form of beauty. While things in the visible world can change and lose their beauty, the Form of beauty is eternal, never changes, and cannot be seen.

Plato believed that concepts like beauty, courage, goodness, temperance, and justice exist in an entire world of Forms, outside of space and time, unaffected by what happens in the visible world.

While the idea of Forms appears in many of Plato's dialogues, Plato's concept of Forms differs from text to text, and sometimes these differences are never completely explained. Through Plato's theory of Forms, Plato incorporates abstract thought as a means to achieve a greater knowledge.

THE TRIPARTITE THEORY OF THE SOUL

In *The Republic* and another well-known dialogue, *Phaedrus*, Plato discusses his understanding of rationality and the soul. The soul, according to Plato, can be broken down into three parts: reason, spirit, and appetite.

1. **Reason:** This is the part of the soul responsible for thinking and understanding when something is true versus false, real versus not apparent, and making rational decisions.
2. **Spirit:** This is the part of the soul responsible for all desires that want victory and honor. If an individual has a just soul, the spirit should enforce reason so that reason leads. Frustration of the spirit will lead to feelings of anger and feeling mistreated.
3. **Appetite:** This is the part of the soul where very basic cravings and desires come from. For example, things like thirst and hunger can be found in this part of the soul. However, the appetite also features unnecessary and unlawful urges, like overeating or sexual excess.

To explain these different parts of the soul, Plato first looked at three different classes in a just society: Guardian, Auxiliary, and Laborers. According to Plato, reason should rule an individual's decisions; spirit should aid reason; and appetite should obey. By maintaining the relationship among these three parts in the correct way, an individual will achieve individual justice.

Similarly, Plato believed that in a perfect society, reason would be represented by a Guardian class (rulers who led based on philosophy, which society would wholeheartedly follow); spirit would be represented by the Auxiliary class (soldiers who would force the rest of society to obey the Guardian class); and appetite would be represented by the Laborers, the workers and merchants of society.

THE IMPORTANCE OF EDUCATION

Plato placed great emphasis on the role of education and believed it to be one of the most important pieces in creating a healthy state. Plato saw the vulnerability of a child's mind and understood how easily it could be molded. He believed children should be taught early on to always seek wisdom and to live a virtuous life. Plato even went so far as to create detailed directions on what exercises a pregnant woman could perform so that she would have a healthy fetus and what types of art and exercise children should immerse themselves in. To Plato, who considered the Athenian people to be corrupt, easily seduced, and gullible to rhetoric, education was essential to having a just society.

PLATO'S CAVE

Knowledge versus the senses

In one of his most well-known texts, *The Republic*, Plato sets out to demonstrate how human perception exists without anyone being aware of the existence of Forms, and how true knowledge is only gained through philosophy. Any knowledge gained by the senses is not knowledge at all, but simply opinion.

Plato's Cave

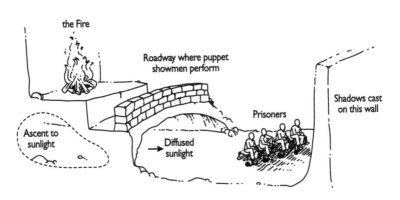

THE ALLEGORY

The Allegory of the Cave reads as a conversation between Socrates and Plato's brother, Glaucon. In the dialogue, Socrates asks Glaucon to imagine a world where an illusion is perceived as reality. To further his point, he creates the following example:

There exists a cave where, inside, a group of prisoners has been locked up since birth. These prisoners cannot move. Their necks and legs are chained so that they can't shift or turn around and they can only see what is in front of them: a stone wall. Behind and above the prisoners is a fire, and between the fire and the prisoners is a low wall where people walk, carrying objects on their heads. The light of the fire casts shadows of the objects onto the wall in front of the prisoners. These shadows are all the prisoners can see. The only sounds they hear are the echoes from the cave.

Now, because these prisoners have never been exposed to the actual objects and all their lives they have only witnessed the shadows, they mistake these shadows for reality. The echoes of the cave, to them, are noises created by the shadows. If a shadow of a book were to appear, for example, these prisoners would claim that they have seen a book. They are not saying this is a shadow of a book, because their reality doesn't know shadows. Eventually, one of the prisoners would understand the nature of this world and would be able to guess what shadow would come next, which would lead to praise and recognition from the other prisoners.

Now, let's suppose one of the prisoners is set free. If a person were to show that prisoner an actual book, the prisoner would not be able to recognize it. To the prisoner, a book is the shadow that was cast on the wall. The illusion of a book seems more real than the book itself.

Socrates continues, pondering what would happen if that freed prisoner were to then turn toward the fire. The prisoner would surely turn away from so much light and turn back to the dark shadows, which he holds to be more real. Now, what if this was taken one step further, and the prisoner was forced to go outside? The prisoner would be angry, distressed, and unable to see the reality before him because he would be so blinded by the light.

If this story sounds vaguely familiar, that's because you might have seen some variation of it before. The 1999 blockbuster movie *The Matrix* is loosely based on Plato's Allegory of the Cave. To quote Keanu Reeves's character Neo, "Whoa."

After a little while, however, the prisoner would adjust and understand that the reality in the cave was incorrect. He would look toward the sun and understand that this entity was what created seasons, years, and everything that was visible in this world (and was even the cause of what he and his fellow prisoners had been seeing in the cave to a certain extent). The prisoner would not look back at those days in the cave with fond memories, for he would now understand that his former perception was not actually reality. The freed prisoner then decides to return to the cave and set the others free. When the prisoner returns, he struggles to adjust to the darkness of the cave. The other prisoners find this behavior startling (for the darkness of the cave is still their only reality), and instead of offering praise, they find him to be stupid and will not believe what the freed prisoner has to say. The prisoners threaten to kill the freed prisoner if he sets them free.

WHAT IT MEANS

Plato compares the prisoners chained inside the cave to people that are unaware of his theory of Forms. People mistake the appearance of what is in front of them as reality and live in ignorance (and quite happily, for ignorance is all these people know). However, when parts of the truth start to emerge, it can be frightening and can make people want to turn back. If one does not turn away from the truth and continues to seek it, he will have a better understanding of the world around him (and will never be able to return to that state of ignorance). The freed prisoner represents the philosopher, seeking a greater truth outside of the perceived reality.

According to Plato, when people use language, they are not naming physical objects that can be seen; rather, they are naming something that can't be seen. These names correlate to things that can only be grasped in the mind. The prisoner believed that the shadow of a book was actually a book until he was finally able to turn around and see the truth. Now, replace the idea of a book with something more substantial, like the notion of justice. Plato's theory of Forms is what allows people to finally turn around and discover the truth. In essence, knowledge gained through the senses and perception is not knowledge at all, but opinion. It is only through philosophical reasoning that one is able to pursue knowledge.

EXISTENTIALISM

The individual and the human experience

Existentialism is not a school of thought so much as a trend that appears throughout philosophy during the nineteenth and twentieth centuries. Prior to this time, philosophical thought had grown to become increasingly more complex and abstract. In dealing with ideas of nature and truth, philosophers began to exclude the importance of human beings.

However, starting with Søren Kierkegaard and Friedrich Nietzsche in the nineteenth century, several philosophers emerged placing a newfound focus on the human experience. Though there are significant differences between philosophers of existentialism (a term that would not be used until the twentieth century), the one common theme among all of them is the notion that philosophy should focus on the experience of human existence in this world. In other words, existentialism seeks out the meaning of life and finding oneself.

COMMON THEMES OF EXISTENTIALISM

Though existentialist thought varies from philosopher to philosopher, there are several common themes. One of the key ideas of existentialism is that the meaning of life and discovering oneself can only be attained by free will, personal responsibility, and choice.

The Individual

Existentialism deals with the question of what it means to exist as a human being. Existentialists believe that humans have been thrown into this universe, and therefore it is existing in this world, and not consciousness, that is the ultimate reality. A person is an individual who has the ability to think and act independently and should be defined by his actual life. It is through an individual's own consciousness that values and purpose are determined.

Choice

Existentialist philosophers believe that all humans have free will. The ability to have free will leads to life choices. Structures and values of society have no control over a person. Personal choices are unique to every individual and are based on outlook, beliefs, and experiences, not external forces or society. Based on these choices, people begin to discover who and what they are. There is no purpose for desires such as wealth, honor, or pleasure, for these are not responsible for having a good life.

The notion of personal responsibility is a key component of existentialism. It is entirely up to the individual to make decisions—and these decisions are not without their own consequences and stress. However, it is in the moments when an individual fights against his very nature that he is at his best. In essence, the very choices we make in life determine our nature, and there are things in this world that are unnatural and irrational.

Anxiety

Existentialists place great emphasis on moments when truths about our existence and nature bring a new awareness into what life means. These existential moments of crisis produce feelings of anxiety, angst, and dread afterward, and are the result of the freedom and independent responsibility we all have.

Because humans have been thrown into this universe, there is a certain meaninglessness to our existence. Our freedom means we are uncertain of the future, and our lives are determined by the choices we make. We believe we have an understanding about the universe around us, and when we discover something that tells us differently, we experience an existential crisis that forces us to re-evaluate aspects of our lives. The only way to have meaning and value is through making choices and taking responsibility.

Authenticity

To be authentic, one must truly be in harmony with his freedom. In existentialism, the notion of authenticity means really coming to terms with oneself, and then living accordingly. One must be able to come to terms with his identity while also not letting his background and history play a part in his decision-making process. Making choices should be done based on one's values, so that there is a responsibility that comes with the decision-making process.

If one does not live within a balance of his freedom, he is inauthentic. It is in the inauthentic experience that people allow ideas like determinism, believing choices are meaningless, and acting as "one should" to persuade their choice-making.

The Absurd

Absurdity is one of the most famous notions affiliated with existentialism. It is often argued in existentialism that there is no reason to exist and that nature has no design. While sciences and metaphysics might be able to provide an understanding of the natural world, these provide more of a description than an actual explanation, and don't provide any insight into meaning or value. According to existentialism, as humans, we should come to terms with this fact and realize that the ability to understand the world is impossible to achieve. The world has no meaning other than the meaning that we provide it.

Furthermore, if an individual makes a choice, it is based on a reason. However, since one can never truly understand meaning, the reasoning is absurd, and so too is the decision to follow through with the choice.

RELIGION AND EXISTENTIALISM

While there are some very famous Christian and Jewish philosophers who use existentialist themes in their work, on the whole, existentialism is commonly associated with atheism. This does not mean that all atheists are necessarily existentialists; rather, those who subscribe to existentialist thought are often atheists.

Why is this the case? Existentialism does not set out to prove that God does or does not exist. Rather, the main ideas and themes of existentialism (such as complete freedom) simply do not mesh well with the notion of there being an omnipotent, omnipresent, omniscient, and omnibenevolent being. Even those existentialists who maintain a belief in a higher being agree that religion is suspicious. Existentialism asks human beings to search and discover their meaning and purpose from within themselves, and this is not possible if they believe in some external force controlling humanity.

ARISTOTLE (384–322 B.C.)

Wisdom starts with understanding yourself

Aristotle was born around 384 B.C. Though little is known about his mother, Aristotle's father was court physician to the Macedonian king Amyntas II (the connection and affiliation with the Macedonian court would continue to play an important role throughout Aristotle's life). Both of Aristotle's parents died when he was young, and at the age of seventeen, Aristotle's guardian sent him to Athens to pursue a higher education. It was in Athens that Aristotle would enroll in Plato's Academy and study under Plato. He would remain there for the next twenty years, studying with Plato as both a student and colleague.

When Plato died in 347 B.C., many believed Aristotle would take his place as director of the Academy. However, by that time, Aristotle had differing views on several of Plato's works (for example, he disagreed with Plato's theory of Forms), and Aristotle was not offered the position.

In 338 B.C., Aristotle returned to Macedonia and began tutoring the thirteen-year-old son of King Philip II, Alexander (later known as "the Great"). When, in 335 B.C., Alexander became king and conquered Athens, Aristotle returned to Athens. While Plato's Academy (which was now directed by Xenocrates) was still the major school in the city, Aristotle decided to create his own school, the Lyceum.

With the death of Alexander the Great in 323 B.C., the government was overthrown and anti-Macedonian sentiment was high. Facing charges of impiety, Aristotle fled Athens to avoid being prosecuted and remained on the island of Euboea until his death in 322 B.C.

LOGIC

While Aristotle focused on many different subjects, one of his most significant contributions to the world of philosophy and Western thought was his creation of logic. To Aristotle, the process of learning could be placed into three distinct categories: theoretical, practical, and productive. Logic, however, did not belong to any one of these categories.

Instead, logic was a tool used to attain knowledge, and was therefore the very first step in the learning process. Logic enables us to discover errors and establish truths.

In his book, *Prior Analytics*, Aristotle introduced the notion of the syllogism, which turned out to be one of the most important contributions to the field of logic. A syllogism is a type of reasoning whereby a conclusion can be deduced based on a series of specific premises or assumptions.

For example:

- All Greek people are human.
- All humans are mortal.
- Therefore, all Greek people are mortal.

To further break down what a syllogism is, one can summarize it in the following way:

- If all X are Y, and all Y are Z, then all X are Z.

Syllogisms are made up of three propositions: the first two are premises; the last is the conclusion. Premises can either be universal (using words like *every*, *all*, or *no*) or particular (for example, using the word *some*), and they can also be affirmative or negative.

Aristotle then set out to create a set of rules that would produce a valid inference. One classic example is:

- At least one premise has to be universal.
- At least one premise has to be affirmative.
- If one of the premises is negative, the conclusion will be negative.

For example:

- No dogs are birds.
- Parrots are birds.
- Therefore, no dogs are parrots.

Aristotle believed three rules applied to all valid thoughts:

1. **The law of identity:** This law states that X is X, and this holds true because X has certain characteristics. A tree is a tree because we can see the leaves, the trunk, the branches, and so on. A tree does not have another identity other than a tree. Therefore, everything that exists has its own characteristics true to itself.
2. **The law of noncontradiction:** This law states X can't be X and not X simultaneously. A statement can never be true and false at the exact same time. If this were the case, a contradiction would arise. If you were to say you fed the cat yesterday and then say you did not feed the cat yesterday, there is a contradiction.
3. **The law of the excluded middle:** This law claims a statement can be either true or false; there cannot be middle ground. This law also claims something has to either be true or be false. If you say your hair is blond, the statement is either true or false. However, later philosophers and mathematicians would dispute this law.

METAPHYSICS

Aristotle rejected Plato's theory of Forms. Instead, Aristotle's response to understanding the nature of being was metaphysics (though he never used this word, instead caling it "first philosophy").

While Plato saw a difference between the intelligible world (made up of thoughts and ideas) and the sensible world (made up of what could visibly be seen) and believed the intelligible world was the only true form of reality, Aristotle believed separating the two would remove all meaning. Instead, Aristotle believed the world was made up of substances that could either be form, matter, or both, and that intelligibility was present in all things and beings.

Aristotle's *Metaphysics* is composed of fourteen books that were later grouped together by editors. It is considered to be one of the greatest works ever produced on the subject of philosophy. Aristotle believed that knowledge was made up of specific truths that people gain from experience, as well as the truths that arise from science and art. Wisdom, as opposed to knowledge, is when one understands the fundamental principles that govern all things (these are the most general truths) and then translates this information into scientific expertise.

Aristotle breaks down how things come to be through four causes:

1. **The material cause:** This explains what something is made of.
2. **The formal cause:** This explains what form something takes.
3. **The efficient cause:** This explains the process of how something comes into being.
4. **The final cause:** This explains the purpose something serves.

While other sciences might study reasons for a particular manifestation of being (for example, a biologist would study humans with regard to them being organisms, while a psychologist would study humans as beings with consciousness), metaphysics examines the reason why there is being in the first place. For this reason, metaphysics is often described as "the study of being qua being" (*qua* is Latin for "in so far as").

VIRTUE

Another one of Aristotle's most impactful works was *Ethics*. According to Aristotle, the purpose of ethics is to discover the purpose of life. Aristotle comes to realize that happiness is the ultimate and final good and that people pursue good things in order to achieve happiness. Aristotle claimed that the way to attain happiness (and therefore the very purpose of life) is through virtue.

Virtue requires both choice and habit. Unlike other ways to attain happiness, such as pleasure or honor, with virtue, when an individual makes a decision, the decision comes from that individual's disposition, which is determined by that person's past choices.

A virtuous choice is, then, the mean between the two most extreme choices. Between acting cold to someone and being overly subservient or attentive is the virtuous choice, friendliness.

To Aristotle, the ultimate type of happiness is living a life of intellectual contemplation, and using reason (which is what separates humans from other animals) is the highest form of virtue. However, for one to achieve such a level of virtue, a person needs the proper social environment, and a proper social environment can only be attained by an appropriate government.

THE SHIP OF THESEUS

When is a ship no longer the same ship?

To understand the classic paradox of the ship of Theseus, one must first understand what a paradox is.

Philosophical Definitions

PARADOX: In philosophy, a paradox is a statement that begins with a premise that seems true; however, upon further investigation, the conclusion ends up proving that the seemingly true premise is actually false.

The first time the ship of Theseus paradox appeared in print was in the writing of the ancient Greek philosopher (and Platonist) Plutarch. Plutarch writes of Theseus (the founder-king of Athens) returning from a long voyage at sea. Throughout the voyage, all of the old, decaying planks of wood the ship was made of were thrown overboard and replaced with new, strong pieces of wood. By the time Theseus and his crew finally returned from their trip, every piece of wood that the ship was made from had been replaced. This leads to the question: Was the ship that they returned on the same ship that they left on, even though it was made of completely different pieces of wood? What if the ship still had one of the original pieces of wood in it? What if there were two pieces of wood still in the ship? Would this change one's answer?

Another way to look at it is this:

If the ship Theseus began his journey on is A, and the ship Theseus ended his journey on is B, then does A = B?

THOMAS HOBBES'S ADDITION

Much later, the famous seventeenth-century philosopher Thomas Hobbes took the paradox one step further.

Now, imagine that following Theseus's ship is a scavenger. As Theseus's crew throws the old pieces of wood overboard, the scavenger takes them out of the water and builds his own ship. Two ships arrive at the port: one with Theseus and his crew, made out of new wood; the other, the scavenger's ship, made entirely out of the old wood that Theseus's crew had thrown overboard. In this scenario, which ship is Theseus's ship?

In this scenario, let's call the boat the scavenger arrived in the letter C.

We know that B ≠ C because two ships land in the harbor and so they clearly cannot be one and the same.

So what makes something the ship of Theseus? Is it the individual parts that the ship is made from? Is it the structure? Is it the history of the ship?

WHERE DO WE GO FROM HERE?

One theory, known as the mereological theory of identity (or MTI), states that the identity of something is dependent upon the identity of that thing's component parts. This theory claims that a necessary condition of identity is that there must be a sameness of parts.

In other words, X = Y if all of the parts of X are also a part of Y and vice versa.

For example, object X is composed of certain components at the beginning of a period of time (t1). If by the end of that period of time (t2), the object (which is now Y) has the same components, then it continued to exist.

In the ship of Theseus paradox, according to MTI, A = C. This means that there are two ships. The ship Theseus began his voyage on is the exact same as the ship the scavenger comes in on (making these one ship), and then there is the ship Theseus came to port in, which was composed of new parts.

However, there is a problem with this conclusion. In this scenario, Theseus would have had to change ships in his journey because he comes to the port in B (which does not equal C). But Theseus never leaves his ship. He leaves on A, comes back on B, and was never aboard two ships (which MTI states there must be).

There might be other possible ways to solve this problem. We can abandon what MTI states altogether and instead claim that A = B. In this scenario, there are still only two ships: the ship Theseus began his journey in (A) and the ship he came back in (B) are considered one, and the scavenger's ship is the second.

This scenario also raises problems. To say that A = B would also imply that B ≠ C and therefore A ≠ C. But one cannot feasibly say this because every part of C is a part of A and vice versa. In addition, A and B do not have any parts in common, and yet we are claiming that they are the same ship.

Another theory that can be applied to the paradox of Theseus's ship is called spatiotemporal continuity (STC). This theory states that an object can have a continuous path in space-time, as long as the change is gradual and the shape and form are preserved. This would allow for the gradual changes that are made to the ship over time.

However, even here we see problems! What if every piece of the ship was packed in individual boxes, shipped all over the world to different locations, then shipped back, and then opened and reassembled? While numerically it may be the same ship, the object does not constantly exist as a ship-like object through space-time (note that MTI does seem to fit in this scenario).

WHAT DOES THE SHIP OF THESEUS MEAN?

Of course, this paradox goes beyond a problem about ships. The ship of Theseus is really about identity and what makes us the people that we are. Parts of ourselves change as the years go by, and yet we still consider ourselves to be the same person.

Is our identity the same because of our structure? If that were the case, if you were to lose a limb or even cut your hair, you wouldn't be you anymore. Is it because of your mind and feelings? If that were the case, are you no longer yourself when you lose memories or have a change of heart? Is it because of the parts we are made up of? Our history?

The ship of Theseus and its implications about what identity is are still discussed to this day.

FRANCIS BACON (1561–1626)

Forever changing the way we look at science

Francis Bacon is one of the most important philosophers to come out of the Renaissance era due to his immense contributions in advancing natural philosophy and scientific methodology.

Bacon was born in London, England, on January 22, 1561. He was the youngest child of his father, Sir Nicholas Bacon, Lord Keeper of the Seal, and his mother, Lady Anne Cooke Bacon, who was the daughter of the knight that tutored Edward VI.

In 1573, when he was just eleven years old, Francis Bacon attended Trinity College, Cambridge. After completing his studies in 1575, Bacon enrolled in a law program the next year. It didn't take him very long to realize that this school was too old-fashioned for his tastes (Bacon recalled that his tutors favored Aristotle, while he was much more interested in the humanistic movement that was spreading across the land due to the Renaissance). Bacon left school and became an assistant to the ambassador in France. In 1579, when his father passed away, Bacon returned to London and resumed studying law, completing his degree in 1582.

In 1584, Francis Bacon was elected to Parliament as a member for Melcombe in Dorsetshire, and he would continue to work in Parliament for the next thirty-six years. Eventually, under James I, Francis Bacon became Lord Chancellor, the highest political office. It was as Lord Chancellor, at the pinnacle of his political career, that Bacon encountered a great scandal that would end his political career entirely, making way for his philosophical pursuits.

In 1621, Francis Bacon, then–Lord Chancellor, was accused of accepting bribes and arrested. Bacon pled guilty to his charges and was fined £40,000 and sentenced to serve a prison sentence in the Tower of London. While his fine was waived and he would only spend four days in prison, Bacon would never be allowed to hold political office or sit in Parliament ever again, thus ending his political life.

It was at this point in Francis Bacon's life that he decided to dedicate the remainder of his life (five years) to philosophy.

THE PHILOSOPHICAL WORK OF FRANCIS BACON

Francis Bacon is perhaps best known for his work in natural philosophy. Unlike Plato (who claimed knowledge could be gained through understanding the meaning of words and content) and Aristotle (who placed emphasis on empirical data), Bacon emphasized observation, experimentation, and interaction and set out to create methods that would rely on tangible proof in an effort to explain sciences.

Bacon's Four Idols

Francis Bacon believed the works of Aristotle (which up to that point, scholastic thinkers had agreed with) actually prevented the ability to think independently and acquire new ideas about nature. Bacon argued that through the advancement of science, the quality of human life could improve, and therefore, people should no longer rely on the work of ancient philosophers. Francis Bacon became so disillusioned with the philosophical thinking of his time that he categorized the thought process of people as four categories of false knowledge, which he referred to as "idols." The four idols were:

1. **Idols of the tribe:** These are the false notions that arise from human nature that are common to everyone. For example, human nature causes people to seek out evidence that supports their own conclusions, causes people to try to have things fit into patterns, and causes beliefs to be affected by what people want to believe.
2. **Idols of the cave:** These are interpretations that come about as a result of individual makeup and disposition. For example, some people might favor similarities while others favor differences, and some might favor notions that support their earlier conclusions.
3. **Idols of the marketplace:** These are false notions that arise from the use of language and words as a means to communicate with one another. For example, words can have a variety of meanings, and people have the ability to name and imagine things that do not actually exist.
4. **Idols of the theater:** Francis Bacon believed that philosophies weren't any better than plays. To Bacon, sophistic philosophy like the work of Aristotle focused more on smart but foolish arguments rather than the natural world; empirical philosophy only focused on a small range of experiments and excluded too many other possibilities; and superstitious philosophy, which was philosophy established by religion and superstition, was a corruption of philosophy. To Francis Bacon, superstitious philosophy was the worst type of false notion.

The Inductive Method

With his belief that knowledge should be pursued and his criticism of present-day philosophies, Francis Bacon set out to create a new and organized method that would eventually become his most impactful contribution to the world of philosophy. In his book,

Novum Organum, he details his inductive, also known as scientific, method.

The inductive method combined the process of carefully observing nature with systematically accumulating data. While the deductive method (like the work of Aristotle) began by using one or more true statements (or axioms) as a base and then attempted to prove other true statements, the inductive method begins by taking observations from nature and attempts to uncover laws and theories pertaining to how nature works. In essence, the deductive method uses logic and the inductive method uses nature.

Bacon's Emphasis on Experiments

Bacon emphasized the importance of experimentation in his work and believed experiments needed to be carefully recorded so that the results could be both reliable and repeatable.

The process of the inductive method is as follows:

1. Accumulate a series of specific empirical observations about the characteristic being investigated.
2. Classify these facts into three categories: instances when the characteristic being investigated is present, instances when it is absent, and instances when it is present in varying degrees.
3. Through careful examination of the results, reject notions that do not seem to be responsible for the occurrence and identify possible causes responsible for the occurrence.

THE COW IN THE FIELD

Challenging the definition of knowledge

Imagine the following scenario:

A farmer worries because his prize cow has wandered away from his farm. A milkman comes to the farm, and the farmer expresses his concern. The milkman tells the farmer he shouldn't worry because he's actually seen the cow in a nearby field. The farmer looks at the field in the distance just to be sure, and he sees what seems to be a large shape that is black and white. The farmer is satisfied by what he has seen and now knows the location of his cow.

Later, the milkman decides to go to the field to double-check that the cow really is there. The cow is in fact in the field, but to the milkman's surprise, the cow is actually completely hidden in a grove of trees. However, in the same field, there is a large black-and-white piece of paper caught in a tree. Upon seeing this, the milkman realizes that the farmer mistook this large piece of paper for his cow.

This then raises the question: Was the farmer right when he said he knew the cow was in the field?

THE GETTIER PROBLEM AND THE TRIPARTITE THEORY OF KNOWLEDGE

The cow in the field is a classic example of what is known as a "Gettier problem." Gettier problems, discovered by Edmund Gettier in 1963, are challenges to the traditional philosophical approach to defining knowledge as a true belief that is justified. Gettier created a series of problems (based on actual or possible situations) where an individual has a belief that ends up being true and has evidence to support it, but it fails to actually be knowledge.

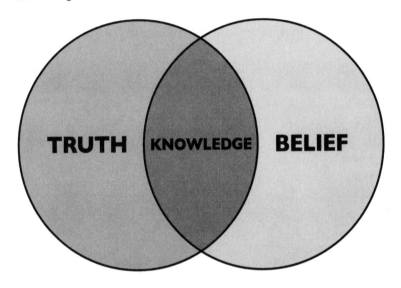

According to Plato, in order for one to have knowledge of something, three conditions have to be satisfied. This is known as the tripartite theory of knowledge.

According to the tripartite theory of knowledge, knowledge is when a true belief is justified. Therefore, if a person believes something to be true, and then it ends up being true through justification, then that person knows it. The three conditions of the tripartite theory of knowledge are:

1. **Belief:** A person can't know something to be true without first believing that it is true.
2. **Truth:** If a person knows something, then it must be true. If a belief is false, then it cannot be true, and therefore, it cannot be known.
3. **Justification:** It is not enough to simply believe something to be true. There must be a justification through sufficient evidence.

With the Gettier problems, Edmund Gettier was able to show that the tripartite theory of knowledge was incorrect. While his problems differed in specific details, they all shared two similar characteristics:

1. While justification is present, the justification is fallible because there is the possibility that the belief could end up being false.
2. Each problem features luck. In all of the Gettier problems, the belief becomes justified; however, it is due to the presence of pure luck.

ATTEMPTS TO SOLVE GETTIER PROBLEMS

There are four main theories that attempt to fix the tripartite theory of knowledge. Now, instead of three conditions (which can be looked at as a triangle), knowledge has an extra condition (and is now viewed as a square).

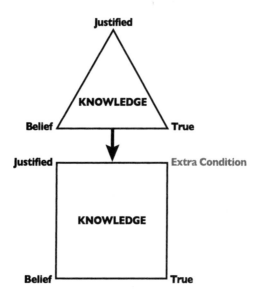

The four main theories are:

1. **No False Belief Condition:** This theory states a belief cannot be based on a belief that is false. For example, a watch stops working at 10 A.M., and you are unaware of this fact. Twelve hours later, at 10 P.M., you look at the watch. The time on the watch is actually correct, but your belief that the watch is working is incorrect.

2. **Causal Connection Condition:** Between knowledge and a belief, there has to be a causal connection. For example, consider the following situation. Tom believes Frank is in his bedroom. Tom sees Frank standing in his bedroom. Therefore, Tom is justified in his belief. Unknown to Tom, however, is the fact that Tom didn't see Frank at all. Instead, it was Frank's twin brother, Sam, who was standing and seen by Tom, and Frank is actually hiding underneath Tom's bed.

While Frank was in the room, it was not because Tom knew this. According to the causal connection condition, Tom shouldn't be able to conclude that Frank is in the bedroom because there is no connection between seeing Sam and knowing Frank is in the room.

3. **Conclusive Reasons Condition:** A reason for a belief must exist that would not exist if the belief itself were false. For example, if a person believes there is a table in front of him, the reason would not exist if there was not a table in front of him.

4. **Defeasibility Condition:** This theory states that as long as there is not evidence pointing to the contrary, a belief is known. In the scenario with Tom, Frank, and Sam, Tom is entitled to say Frank is in the bedroom because he isn't aware of evidence pointing to the contrary.

While these four theories attempt to fix the tripartite theory of knowledge, they also have their problems. It is for this reason that Edmund Gettier's work has become so influential. From his work, the question arises: Will we ever truly understand knowledge?

DAVID HUME (1711–1776)

One of the most important contributors to Western philosophy

David Hume was born to a modest family in Edinburgh, Scotland, in 1711. At the age of two, Hume's father died and his mother was left to care for him and his brother and sister. At the age of twelve, Hume was sent to the University of Edinburgh, where he developed a passion for classics and spent the next three years studying philosophy and trying to create his own philosophical program.

His studies proved to be extraordinarily taxing on Hume, and it began to compromise his psychological health. After working for a short time as a clerk for a sugar importer, Hume finally recovered and moved to France to continue working on his own philosophical vision. Between 1734 and 1737, while living in La Flèche, France, Hume wrote one of his most impactful philosophical works, *A Treatise of Human Nature*. This work was later published in England as three books between 1739 and 1740, with Hume removing parts that would seem controversial for the time (such as his discussion of miracles).

Hume wanted to work in the British academic system. His *Treatise* was poorly received, however, and while his next two-volume compilation, *Essays, Moral, Political, and Literary*, was modestly successful, Hume's reputation for being an atheist and skeptic ruined any chances of a career in education.

A TREATISE OF HUMAN NATURE

Hume's most influential work was broken down into three books and covered a wide range of philosophical subjects.

Book I: Of the Understanding

Hume argues that empiricism, the notion that all knowledge comes from experiences, is valid and that ideas are essentially no different from experiences because complex ideas are the result of simpler ideas, and the simpler ideas were formed from the impressions our senses created. Hume then also argues that when something is a "matter of fact," it is a matter that has to be experienced and cannot be arrived at through instinct or reason.

With these arguments, Hume takes on the notion of God's existence, divine creation, and the soul. According to Hume, since people cannot experience or get an impression from God, divine creation, or the soul, there is no real reason to believe in their existence.

It is in his first book that Hume introduces three tools used for philosophical inquiry: the microscope, the razor, and the fork.

- **Microscope:** In order to understand an idea, one must first break down the idea into the simplest ideas that it is made up of.
- **Razor:** If a term cannot come from an idea that can be broken down into simpler ideas, then that term has no meaning. Hume uses the notion of the razor to devalue ideas such as metaphysics and religion.
- **Fork:** This is the principle that truths can be separated into two types. One type of truth states that once ideas (such as a true statement in math) are proven, they remain proven. The other truth relates to matters of fact and things that occur in the world.

Book II: Of the Passions

In Hume's second book, he focuses on what he refers to as passions (feelings like love, hatred, grief, joy, etc.). Hume classifies passions like he classifies ideas and impressions. He first makes a distinction between original impressions, which are received through the senses, and secondary impressions, which come from original impressions.

Original impressions are internal and from physical sources. They appear in the form of physical pains and pleasures and are new to us because they come from physical sources. According to Hume, the passions are found in the world of secondary impressions. Hume then makes the distinction between direct passions (like grief, fear, desire, hope, joy, and aversion) and indirect passions (like love, hatred, pride, and humility).

Hume states that morality is not based on reason because moral decisions affect actions, while decisions made from reason do not. An individual's beliefs in regard to cause and effect are beliefs relating to the connections among objects that people experience. The actions of an individual are affected only when the objects are of interest, and they are only of interest to people if they have the ability to cause pain or pleasure.

Therefore, Hume argues, pleasure and pain are what motivate people and create passions. Passions are feelings that initiate actions, and reason should act as a "slave" to passion. Reason can influence an individual's actions in two ways: It directs passions to focus on objects, and it discovers the connections among events that will eventually create passions.

Book III: Of Morals

Based on the ideas he set forth in his first two books, Hume takes on the notion of morality. First, Hume distinguishes between virtue and vice. Hume claims these moral distinctions are impressions, not ideas. While the impression of virtue is pleasure, the impression of vice is pain. These moral impressions are only the result of human action and cannot be caused by inanimate objects or animals.

Hume argues that an individual's actions are only determined to be moral or immoral based on how they affect others (and not how they affect the individual). Therefore, moral impressions should only be considered from a social point of view. With this notion in mind, Hume claims that the foundation of moral obligation is sympathy.

Morality is not a matter of fact that is the result of experience. Hume uses murder as an example. If one were to examine murder, one would not experience pain, and therefore, one couldn't find the vice. You would only uncover your own dislike of murder. This shows that morality does not exist in reason, but rather, in passions.

Because of David Hume's criticism of philosophical theories, ideas, and methodologies that relied heavily on rationalism, he became one of the most important minds in Western philosophy. His work touched on an incredible number of philosophical topics, including religion, metaphysics, personal identity, morality, and concepts of cause-effect relations.

HEDONISM

It's all about pleasure and pain

The term *hedonism* actually refers to several theories that, while different from one another, all share the same underlying notion: Pleasure and pain are the only important elements of the specific phenomena the theories describe. In philosophy, hedonism is often discussed as a theory of value. This means that pleasure is the only thing intrinsically valuable to a person at all times and pain is the only thing that is intrinsically not valuable to an individual. To hedonists, the meaning of pleasure and pain is broad so that it can relate to both mental and physical phenomena.

ORIGINS AND HISTORY OF HEDONISM

The first major hedonistic movement dates back to the fourth century B.C. with the Cyrenaics, a school of thought founded by Aristippus of Cyrene. The Cyrenaics emphasized Socrates' belief that happiness is one of the results of moral action, but also believed that virtue had no intrinsic value. They believed that pleasure, specifically physical pleasure over mental pleasure, was the ultimate good and that immediate gratification was more desirable than having to wait a long time for pleasure.

Following the Cyrenaics was Epicureanism (led by Epicurus), which was a form of hedonism quite different from that of Aristippus. While he agreed that pleasure was the ultimate good, Epicurus believed that pleasure was attained through tranquility and a reduction of desire instead of immediate gratification. According to Epicurus, living a simple life full of friends and philosophical discussion was the highest pleasure that could be attained.

During the Middle Ages, hedonism was rejected by Christian philosophers because it did not mesh with Christian virtues and ideals, such as faith, hope, avoiding sin, and helping others. Still, some philosophers argued hedonism had its merits because it was God's desire that people be happy.

Hedonism was most popular in the eighteenth and nineteenth centuries due to the work of Jeremy Bentham and John Stuart Mill, who both argued for variations of prudential hedonism, hedonistic utilitarianism, and motivational hedonism.

VALUE AND PRUDENTIAL HEDONISM

In philosophy, hedonism usually refers to value and well-being. Value hedonism states that pleasure is the only thing that is intrinsically valuable, while pain is the only thing that is intrinsically invaluable.

Philosophical Definitions

INTRINSICALLY VALUABLE: The word *intrinsically* is thrown around a lot when discussing hedonism, and it is a very important word to understand. Unlike the word *instrumental*, use of the word *intrinsically* implies that something is valuable on its own. Money is instrumentally valuable. Having money only has real value when you purchase something with it. Therefore, it is not intrinsically valuable. Pleasure, on the other hand, is intrinsically valuable. When a person experiences pleasure, even if it does not lead to something else, the initial pleasure itself is enjoyable.

According to value hedonism, everything that is of value is reduced to pleasure. Based on this information, prudential hedonism then goes one step further and claims that all pleasure, and only pleasure, can make an individual's life better, and that all pain, and only pain, can make an individual's life worse.

PSYCHOLOGICAL HEDONISM

Psychological hedonism, also known as motivational hedonism, is the belief that the wish to experience pleasure and avoid pain, both consciously and unconsciously, is responsible for all human behavior. Variations of psychological hedonism have been argued by Sigmund Freud, Epicurus, Charles Darwin, and John Stuart Mill.

Strong psychological hedonism (that is to say, absolutely all behavior is based on avoiding pain and gaining pleasure) has generally been dismissed by today's philosophers. There is countless evidence to show that this is just simply not the case (like when a seemingly painful act is done out of a sense of duty), and it is generally accepted that decisions can be made based on motives that do not involve seeking pleasure or staying away from pain.

NORMATIVE HEDONISM

Normative hedonism, also known as ethical hedonism, is a theory that states that happiness should be sought out. Here, the definition of happiness is "pleasure minus pain." Normative hedonism is used to argue theories that deal with explaining how and why an action can be morally permissible or impermissible.

Normative hedonism can be broken down into two types, which use happiness to decide whether an action is morally right or wrong:

1. **Hedonistic Egoism:** This theory states that people should act in the way that best suits their own interests, which would, in effect, make them happy. Consequences do not have to be considered (and have no value) for anyone other than the individual performing the action. However, under hedonistic egoism, desensitization needs to occur. If a person steals to suit his own interest, he should feel no difference between stealing from a rich or poor person.

2. **Hedonistic Utilitarianism:** This theory states that an action is right (morally permissible) when it produces or most likely produces the largest net happiness for everyone that it concerns. Utilitarianism thus pertains to the happiness of everyone who could be affected and not just an individual (everyone is given equal weight). According to hedonistic utilitarianism, stealing from the poor would be morally impermissible because it would leave the poor person unhappy and the thief would only be slightly happier (and if he feels guilty, his happiness is even less).

Though hedonistic utilitarianism seems like an appealing theory because it treats everybody equally, it has faced criticism for holding no intrinsic moral value to things like friendship, justice, truth, etc.

Consider this example: A child is murdered in a small town. The town believes your best friend is the murderer, but you know he is innocent. If the only way to promote the greatest happiness for everyone is to kill your best friend, according to hedonistic utilitarianism, you should do so. It doesn't matter that the killer is still out there—all that matters is the largest net happiness, which would be realized by killing whoever the town believes is the suspect.

PRISONER'S DILEMMA

What choice is the right choice?

The prisoner's dilemma is one of the most famous illustrations of why people might act the way they do. The prisoner's dilemma is actually a part of game theory, a field in mathematics that looks at various outcomes from situations that require strategy. However, the prisoner's dilemma goes far beyond simply being a mathematical notion. It raises important questions about morality, psychology, and philosophy, and can even be observed in the real world.

THE ORIGINS OF THE PRISONER'S DILEMMA

In 1950, RAND Corporation hired mathematicians Merrill Flood and Melvin Dresher as part of their ongoing investigation into game theory and how it could be applied to global nuclear strategy. Based on the puzzles that Flood and Dresher created, Princeton professor Albert W. Tucker tweaked their work to make it more accessible to the masses, thus creating what is now known as the prisoner's dilemma.

THE PRISONER'S DILEMMA

Two prisoners, prisoner A and prisoner B, are taken into custody. The police do not have a sufficient amount of evidence, so they decide to put A and B in separate rooms. The police officers tell each prisoner that if he turns in the other person and the other person remains silent, he will be able to go free while the prisoner who remained silent will face jail time. If both A and B confess, they will both have to face some jail time (though a shorter sentence than the one faced by the person who did not speak). If both prisoner A and B remain silent, they will both face an even shorter prison sentence.

For example:

	Confess A	Stay Quiet A
Confess B	6 / 6	10 / 0
Stay Quiet B	0 / 10	2 / 2

According to this diagram, if prisoner A and prisoner B both confess, they will each have to serve six years. If prisoner A remains quiet while prisoner B confesses (which implicates prisoner A in the process), prisoner A has to serve ten years while prisoner B can go home. Likewise, if prisoner A confesses but prisoner B remains quiet, then prisoner A can go home while prisoner B faces ten years in prison. Lastly, if both remain quiet, they will each face two years. Another way we can view this is:

	C	D
C	R,R	S,T
D	T,S	P,P

C represents a player cooperating (in this case, remaining silent) and D represents a player defecting (confessing). R stands for the reward that the players would receive if both decided to cooperate; P represents the punishment both players would receive for defecting; T is the temptation that a player would have for defecting alone; and lastly, S represents the "sucker" payoff that the player would have for cooperating alone.

WHAT IT MEANS

The dilemma in the prisoner's dilemma is this: Prisoner A and prisoner B are better off confessing; however, the outcome from having them both confess is much worse than it would have been if both had remained silent.

Prisoner's dilemma is a perfect illustration of the conflict that arises between group rationality and individual rationality. If a group of people act rationally, they will actually do far worse than if a group of people acted irrationally. In the prisoner's dilemma, it is assumed that all players are rational and know that the other player involved is rational. The rational thought would be to defect. But by choosing to protect themselves and acting in their own interest, the prisoners will actually be worse off.

MULTIPLE MOVES

Now, let's add another option to the game. Players now have the option to defect, cooperate, or neither (N). We now see that defecting is no longer the dominant choice, and that the players will actually fare better by choosing to cooperate if the other player chooses neither.

	C	**D**	**N**
C	R,R	S,T	T,S
D	T,S	P,P	R,S
N	S,T	S,R	S,S

MULTIPLE PLAYERS AND THE TRAGEDY OF THE COMMONS

The structure of prisoner's dilemma can appear in grander settings, such as big groups or even societies. It is here that we see how morality comes into effect. Perhaps the best example to showcase a multiplayer prisoner's dilemma is a situation known as the "tragedy of the commons."

In the tragedy of the commons, a group of neighboring farmers all prefer that their cows not graze on their own individual properties (which are not very suitable), but on the commons. However, if the commons reaches a certain threshold, the land will become unsuitable for grazing. By acting rationally (in their own self-interest) and trying to reap the benefits of the land, the farmers will deplete the land and create a negative impact for everyone. Like prisoner's dilemma, an individual rational strategy creates irrational outcomes that affect the group.

So what do the prisoner's dilemma and tragedy of the commons tell us about morality? Essentially, these examples prove that pursuing one's own self-interest and gratification will actually turn out to be self-defeating in the long run.

EXAMPLE OF PRISONER'S DILEMMA IN THE REAL WORLD

A classic example of the prisoner's dilemma in the real world is currently a major issue in today's fishing industry. Currently, industrial fishermen are catching fish at an extremely fast rate. While this might seem like it is good for current profits, the rate at which these fish are being caught is faster than the amount of time needed for the fish to reproduce. As a result, the fishermen now have a depleted supply of fish to choose from, thus creating a hardship for all fishermen.

In order to ensure the livelihood of the industry in the long term, fishermen should cooperate with one another and forgo high profits in the immediate future (thus, going against their own self-interest).

ST. THOMAS AQUINAS (1225–1274)

Philosophy and religion

Thomas Aquinas was born around 1225 in Lombardy, Italy, to the Countess of Teano. When he was just five years old, Aquinas was sent to the monastery Montecassino to study with Benedictine monks. He would remain there until the age of thirteen, when, due to great political unrest, Montecassino became a battle site and he was forced to leave.

Aquinas was then transferred to Naples, where he studied at a Benedictine house that was affiliated with the University of Naples. There, he spent the next five years learning about the work of Aristotle and became very interested in contemporary monastic orders. In particular, Aquinas became drawn to the idea of living a life of spiritual service, as opposed to the more traditional and sheltered lifestyle he was accustomed to seeing with the monks at Montecassino.

Thomas Aquinas began to attend the University of Naples around 1239. By 1243, he had joined an order of Dominican monks in secret, and received the habit in 1244. When his family learned of this, they kidnapped him, held him captive for a year, and tried to make him see the error of his ways. Their attempt did not work, however, and when he was released in 1245, Aquinas returned to the Dominican order. Between 1245 and 1252, Aquinas studied with the Dominicans in Naples, Paris, Cologne (where he was ordained in 1950), and eventually returned to Paris to teach theology at the University of Paris.

At a time when the Catholic Church had an overwhelming amount of power and people struggled with the notion of having philosophy and religion coexist, Thomas Aquinas brought faith and reasoning together. He believed that knowledge, whether obtained through nature or through religious studies, all came from God and could work together.

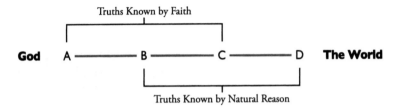

PROOFS FOR THE EXISTENCE OF GOD

Throughout his life, Aquinas wrote an incredible number of philosophical texts that touched on many different subjects, ranging anywhere from natural philosophy and the work of Aristotle to theology and the Bible. His most famous and extensive work, *Summa Theologiae*, provides the most detail in terms of Aquinas's philosophical views. Aquinas began *Summa Theologiae* sometime after 1265 and wrote it until his death in 1274.

Summa Theologiae is broken up into three parts, with each part featuring its own subdivisions. It is in Part 1 that Aquinas's most famous philosophical text, the Five Ways, is found. In this, Thomas Aquinas sets out to prove the existence of God.

Aquinas begins by acknowledging that though philosophy is not a requirement in promoting God's knowledge, it can help theology. He then tries to answer the following questions:

1. Is "God exists" self-evident?
2. Can this be demonstrated?
3. Does God exist?

Aquinas then provides five proofs that show the existence of God. With his Five Ways, Thomas Aquinas combines the ideas of theology with rational thought and observations from the natural world, in order to prove the existence of God.

Proof 1: The Argument of the Unmoved Mover

We can see that there are things in this world that are in motion. Anything that is in motion was put in motion by something else that was in motion. And that object is in motion because it was put into motion by another object that was in motion, and so on and so forth. However, this cannot infinitely keep going backward because there would never be an original mover (and thus, there would never be the subsequent movement). So there must be an unmoved mover that is first, and that is understood to be God.

Proof 2: The Argument of the First Cause

Everything is caused by something, and nothing can be caused by itself. Every cause is the result of a previous cause, and that previous cause was the result of another previous cause. This cannot infinitely keep going backward because if there is no initial cause, then there are no subsequent causes. So there must be an uncaused first cause, which is understood to be God.

Proof 3: The Argument from Contingency

We observe in nature that things come to exist and then cease to exist. However, everything that exists needs to come from something that exists, and if it is possible for something to not exist, then it wouldn't exist before, and it wouldn't exist now. So there must be a being whose existence does not rely on the existence of others, and this is understood to be God.

Proof 4: The Argument from Degree

We observe that beings have varying degrees of characteristics (more good, less good, more noble, less noble, etc.). These varying degrees are being compared to a maximum (the noblest, the best, etc.), and according to Aristotle, the greatest state of being is when there is the greatest state of truth (the maximum). So there has to be a cause to the perfections we find in beings, and this perfection or maximum is understood to be God.

Proof 5: The Teleological Argument

We observe unintelligent and inanimate objects in nature acting toward a purpose, even if these objects are not aware of this fact (such as the food chain or the processes of sensory organs). Though unaware, these objects are clearly acting toward a purpose according to a specific plan, and therefore, there must be a being guiding them that has the knowledge to direct them toward their purpose. This is understood to be God.

ETHICS AND THE CARDINAL VIRTUES

In the second part of *Summa Theologiae*, Aquinas creates a system of ethics based on the work of Aristotle. Like Aristotle, Aquinas believed that a good life is described by attempting to reach the highest end. And like Aristotle, Aquinas also spoke of virtue. To Aquinas, there were cardinal virtues that all other forms of virtue came from. These were justice, prudence, courage, and temperance.

While these cardinal virtues are a template for a moral life, according to Aquinas, they are not enough for one to reach true fulfillment. While Aristotle believed that the highest end was happiness and that the way to achieve this was through virtue,

Aquinas believed the highest end was eternal blessedness, which was achieved by a union with God in the afterlife. It is by living through these cardinal virtues that one moves toward true fulfillment.

Aquinas made a distinction between an eternal happiness that could only be reached in the afterlife, and an imperfect happiness that could be reached in this life. Because eternal happiness is a union with God, there is only an imperfect happiness in this life since we can never know everything there is to know about God in this life.

THE IMPACT OF ST. THOMAS AQUINAS

Thomas Aquinas had an incredible impact on Western philosophy. During his lifetime, the church was extremely influenced by the works of Plato and had dismissed the importance of Aristotle. Aquinas, however, came to realize just how important Aristotle was and incorporated Aristotle's work into Catholic orthodoxy, forever changing the shape of Western philosophy. In 1879, the teachings of Thomas Aquinas became incorporated into official church doctrine by Pope Leo XIII.

HARD DETERMINISM

There is no free will

Hard determinism is the philosophical theory that, because every event has a cause, all human action is predetermined and therefore choices made by free will do not exist. Though the assertion of the hard determinist that nothing can occur without a cause may seem rational, the conclusion that no one ever acts freely has sparked much debate in the philosophical world.

THE FOUR PRINCIPLES OF FREE WILL AND DETERMINISM

In order to better understand hard determinism, it is necessary to analyze four general principles involved in the discussion of free will and determinism:

1. **The Principle of Universal Causation:** This states that every event has a cause. In other words, if "X causes Y" is true, then X and Y are events; X precedes Y; and if X happens, Y has to happen.
2. **The Free Will Thesis:** This states that sometimes people act freely.
3. **The Principle of Avoidability and Freedom:** If a person acts freely, then he could have done something other than what he in fact did. Yet, if no one could have done anything other than what he in fact did, then no one ever acts freely.
4. **The Auxiliary Principle:** This asserts that if every event has a cause, then no one could have done anything other than what he in fact did.

Therefore, if sometimes a person could have done something other than what he in fact did, then some events are uncaused.

Though all four principles initially appear to be intuitively plausible and a case can be made for believing each, it is ultimately apparent that they are incompatible with one another. In other words, not all principles can be true. Much philosophical debate has subsequently been dedicated to determining which of these principles are true and which are false.

Hard determinism responds to this incompatibility of the principles by accepting the principle of universal causation, the principle of avoidability and freedom, and the auxiliary principle as true and rejecting the free will thesis as false:

- **Premise 1:** Every event has a cause (principle of universal causation).
- **Premise 2:** If every event has a cause, then no one could have done anything other than what he in fact did (auxiliary principle, part one).
- **Premise 3:** If no one could have done anything other than what he in fact did, then no one ever acts freely (principle of avoidability and freedom, part two).
- Therefore, no one ever acts freely (denial of free will theory).

Premise 1 is the thesis of determinism: Every event is subject to the law of causality. The rationale for this premise is its appeal to common sense; it seems impossible to even imagine what it would mean for an event to be "uncaused." Premise 2 defines causality: If an event is caused, then it must happen. If it must happen, then nothing else could have happened instead. Premise 3 simply expresses what is meant by "free." Surely if an act must occur, the person committing the act has no choice and is thus not acting freely.

ARGUMENTS AGAINST HARD DETERMINISM

Following are several angles used to try to disprove hard determinism.

Argument from Choice

One argument against hard determinism is the "argument from choice." It is stated as such:

- **Premise 1:** Sometimes we do what we choose to do.
- **Premise 2:** If sometimes we do what we choose to do, then sometimes we are acting freely.
- **Premise 3:** If sometimes we are acting freely, then hard determinism is false.
- Therefore, hard determinism is false.

Premise 1 defines choice as a decision or mental event, and its rationale is simple observation; we see people making choices every day. For example, people choose what clothes to wear, what food to eat, what time to wake up, etc. Premise 2 defines "acting freely" as choosing what we do. If someone chooses to do something, the fact that he is making a choice means that he is acting freely. Premise 3 is the negation of hard determinism.

Because the "argument from choice" is a valid argument, it seems at first to be a solid objection to hard determinism. Further analysis of its definition of acting freely, however, demonstrates the argument to be unsound. Because the "argument from choice" does not deny that events are caused, each assertion that it makes is subject to the laws of causality. With this in mind, it becomes clear that the main problem with the argument is its leap from the first premise to the second.

Though people do, indeed, make what appear to be choices about various aspects of their lives, it does not follow that they are acting freely. A choice is a caused event. Therefore, a person's choice to act in some way is not, itself, the sole or first cause of that action; it is, rather, the last event in a set of conditions that causes the action. A person may choose to wear a red shirt, but his choice to do so is, itself, causally determined. Though the causes for a person's choice are "internal and invisible" and sometimes unknown, they do very much exist. A person's brain had to react in exactly the way it reacted because the choice it made was a determined event. According to philosopher Paul Rée, the person chooses to wear a red shirt because of "causes whose historical development could be traced back ad infinitum." Even if a person thinks he could have done otherwise, it is only under a different, though perhaps very slightly different, set of conditions or causes that he could have acted in a different manner. Therefore, because a choice is a caused event, it is predetermined and must happen. Because the choice must happen, it is not an act of free will.

Argument from Drive Resistance

A second argument against hard determinism is the "argument from drive resistance." It is stated as such:

- **Premise 1:** Sometimes we resist our passions.
- **Premise 2:** If sometimes we resist our passions, then sometimes we are acting freely.

- **Premise 3:** If sometimes we are acting freely, then hard determinism is false.
- Therefore, hard determinism is false.

Premise 1 is a simple observation; people have passions or desires to, for example, commit murder, engage in adultery, or drive recklessly. People, however, are able to prevent themselves from engaging in such activities. Premise 2 gives a definition of "acting freely." A person acts freely if he is able to choose to act in a way that does not yield to passions. This premise suggests that by resisting passions, people are able to avoid the infinite number of historical causes and to ultimately act freely. Premise 3 is the negation of hard determinism.

Like the "argument from choice," the "argument from drive resistance" does not deny that every event has a cause and for this reason is valid but unsound. The strongest objection to this argument is to deny Premise 2; though people are able to resist their passions, it does not follow that they are acting freely. For example, a person may resist the desire to commit murder. However, just as committing a murder has a cause, so too does *not* committing a murder. The person may resist the desire to murder because another desire, such as not wanting to be punished for his actions, pitying the fate of his victim, etc., causes him to do so. A person can never resist all of his drives. By the definition of *free will* given by the "argument from drive resistance," therefore, a person is never acting freely. Additionally, resistance is equally subject to the laws of causality. It is not merely the cause of not murdering; it is an event and thus the effect of some other cause. If a person happens to resist committing murder, he was predetermined to resist committing murder and could not have acted in any other way. Ultimately, resisting one's drives does not free a person from the laws of causality.

Argument from Moral Responsibility

The third argument against hard determinism is the "argument from moral responsibility." It is stated as such:

- **Premise 1:** Sometimes we are morally responsible for our actions.
- **Premise 2:** If sometimes we are morally responsible for our actions, then sometimes we are acting freely.
- **Premise 3:** If sometimes we are acting freely, then hard determinism is false.
- Therefore, hard determinism is false.

The argument defines moral responsibility in this way: X is morally responsible for action A if X deserves praise or blame for doing A. Premise 1 is a simple observation; it appeals to our common sense that if a person commits murder, he should be blamed and punished. If, on the other hand, a person saves another person's life, he should be praised for doing so. Premise 2 defines "acting freely." If people deserve praise or blame for an action, it is only rational that they must have freely chosen to act in the way that they did. For, if they had not acted freely, then they would not be praised or blamed. Premise 3 is a negation of hard determinism.

The "argument from moral responsibility," like the two arguments before it, is valid yet unsound. It presupposes that to "deserve" praise or blame for an action, a person must be the only cause of that action. In other words, a person does not "deserve" praise if he is forced into (by the cause) an act of kindness and does not "deserve" blame if he is forced into an act of cruelty. However, because this argument accepts that events are caused, it must also accept that actions that seem to deserve praise or blame are, themselves, caused events; a person cannot be the sole cause of an event.

The main problem with this argument, therefore, is its first premise; though there are circumstances under which it may seem logical to praise or blame a person, it is actually not the case that a person is ever actually morally responsible for his actions. If a person commits murder, he had no choice but to commit murder. The murder was a caused event and had to happen. If the murder had to happen, then the murderer does not deserve praise or blame for his action. To argue in favor of moral responsibility, therefore, would be to claim that some events are uncaused, a notion that goes against our common sense.

Many philosophers have responded to the rejection of Premise 1 by highlighting the implications it has for our current justice system. If we are to deny that moral responsibility exists, they say, then we have no justification for punishment and we must, therefore, abolish the use of any prison or detention center. A hard determinist would see this conclusion as rash; though moral responsibility may not exist, there are certainly other deserving justifications for punishment. For instance, the prison system can serve as a safety precaution, a violence deterrent, a center for rehabilitation, or to satisfy victim grievances. The very fact that events are caused allows for the belief that prisons may well be the cause of a reduction in violence. The desire not to be punished could be an event in a set of conditions that prevents a person from killing another person.

Hard determinism asserts that nothing happens without a cause, that no act is free from the law of causality. Though there are many arguments against this theory, they ultimately fail to disprove hard determinism.

JEAN-JACQUES ROUSSEAU (1712–1778)

Freedom fighter

Jean-Jacques Rousseau was born on June 28, 1712, in Geneva, Switzerland. Rousseau's mother died soon after his birth, and by the age of twelve, abandoned by his father, Rousseau traveled from home to home, staying with family members, employers, patrons, and lovers. Around 1742, Rousseau, who was now living in Paris and working as a music teacher and music copier, befriended Diderot, one of the major figures of the Enlightenment. Eventually, Rousseau would also become known as a key figure of the Enlightenment, though his relationship with its ideals and others associated with the movement were complex.

Rousseau's first recognition came in 1750, with his *Discourse on the Sciences and Arts.* The Academy of Dijon held an essay contest based on the question of whether or not the restoration of the sciences and arts had the tendency to purify morals, and Rousseau, who won the prize, argued that morals and goodness were corrupted by the advancement of civilization (an idea that would be common throughout his later philosophical texts). Rousseau continued to produce noteworthy texts (such as his famous political text, *Discourse on the Origin of Inequality*) and grew in popularity. In 1762, however, his popularity came crashing down with the publication of his books *The Social Contract* and *Èmile.* The books were met with great controversy and outcry, which included public burnings in Paris and Geneva, and the French monarchy ordered his arrest. Rousseau fled France and ultimately resided in the Swiss town of

Neuchâtel, where he not only renounced his Genevan citizenship but also started working on his famous autobiography, *Confessions*.

Rousseau eventually returned to France and sought refuge with British philosopher David Hume. On July 2, 1778, Rousseau died suddenly. In 1794, during the French Revolution, the new revolutionary government, whose views were vastly different than the monarchy's, ordered that Rousseau's ashes were to be placed in the Pantheon in Paris, and that he was to be honored as a national hero.

The common theme throughout most of Jean-Jacques Rousseau's important philosophical work relates to the ideas of freedom, morality, and the state of nature. His work laid the foundations of the French and American Revolutions and had an incredible impact on Western philosophy.

DISCOURSE ON THE ORIGIN OF INEQUALITY

In one of his most famous political/philosophical texts, *Discourse on the Origin of Inequality*, Jean-Jacques Rousseau explains the essential elements of his philosophy. First, Rousseau lays out the different types of inequality that exist for people. He then takes these types of inequality and tries to determine which are "natural" and which are "unnatural" (meaning they could therefore be prevented).

Rousseau believed that man, like every other animal found in nature, is motivated by two principles: self-preservation and pity. In man's natural state, man is happy, needs little, and knows nothing of good and evil. The only thing that separates man from any other animal is a sense (though unrealized) of perfectability.

It is this idea of perfectability that allows man to change over time. As humans socialize with other humans, the mind develops and reason begins to form. However, socialization also leads to a principle Rousseau refers to as "*amour propre*," which is what drives humans to compare themselves to one another and seek domination over other humans in order to create happiness.

As human societies become more complex and *amour propre* develops further, things like private property and labor are divided amongst the people, and this allows for the exploitation of the poor. The poor will then seek to end such discrimination by starting a war with the rich. However, the rich deceive the poor by creating a political society claiming to provide equality. Equality is not provided, however, and instead, oppression and inequality become permanent fixtures in society.

Rousseau's Natural Inequalities

According to Rousseau, the only natural inequalities are differences in physical strength, because these are inequalities that arise in the natural state. In modern society, man is corrupted, and the inequalities that result from laws and property are not natural and should not be tolerated.

THE SOCIAL CONTRACT

Jean-Jacques Rousseau is perhaps best known for his book *The Social Contract*, where he famously said, "Men are born free, yet everywhere are in chains." According to Rousseau, when man came into society, he had complete freedom and equality. Yet civil society acts as chains and suppresses man's inherent freedom.

To Rousseau, the only legitimate form of political authority is one in which all people have agreed upon a government with the intent of mutual preservation through a social contract. Rousseau refers to this group of people as a "sovereign." The sovereign should always express the collective need of the people and provide for the common good of everyone, regardless of individual opinions or desires (he calls this the "general will"). The general will also shapes the creation of laws.

Rousseau does not dismiss the importance of government, however, and understood that there would be friction between a sovereign and a government (whether it be a monarchy, aristocracy, or democracy). To ease such tensions, Rousseau claimed the sovereign should hold periodic assemblies and vote based on the general will. The assemblies should always be attended by the people of the sovereign, for the sovereignty is lost once elected representatives attend the assemblies, and in a truly healthy state, the votes should be practically unanimous. Furthermore, Rousseau advocates that there should be a court to mediate conflicts among individuals, and among the government and the sovereignty.

Jean-Jacques Rousseau's *The Social Contract* is one of the most important philosophical texts in Western philosophy. At a time of political inequality, Rousseau made it clear that the right of the government was to govern by "the consent of the governed." His radical ideas regarding the rights of man and the sovereignty of the people are frequently acknowledged as being the foundations of human rights and democratic principles.

THE TROLLEY PROBLEM

Facing the consequences

Imagine the following scenario:

A trolley has lost control of its brakes, and the driver has no way of stopping the train as it hurtles down the tracks on a very steep hill. A bit farther down the hill, you are standing and watching the episode unfold. You notice that a little farther down from where you are standing, five workmen stand on the tracks. The trolley is headed right for them. If something is not done, these five men will surely die.

Right next to you, you notice there is a lever that will make the trolley move onto another track. However, upon looking at this second track, you see that there is one person on it. If you switch the direction of the trolley, the five workers from the first track will survive; however, the one person on the second track will die. What do you do?

Now imagine this scenario:

You are standing on a bridge and watch as a trolley loses control and hurtles down the hill. At the end of the tracks are the five workmen who are bound to die. This time, there is no lever to move the trolley to another track. The trolley will be passing under the bridge that you are standing on, though, and you know that dropping a heavy weight in front of the trolley will make it stop. You happen to be standing next to a very fat man and realize that the only way to stop the trolley from killing the five workmen is by pushing the fat man over the bridge and onto the track, which, as a result, will kill the fat man. What do you do?

The trolley problem, which continues to be a source of debate to this day, was first introduced in 1967 by British philosopher Philippa Foot and was later expanded upon by American philosopher Judith Jarvis Thomson.

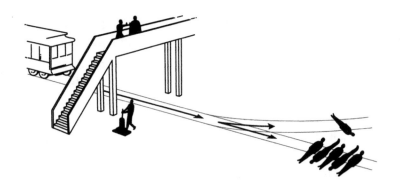

CONSEQUENTIALISM

The trolley problem is a perfect critique of consequentialism. Consequentialism is the philosophical view that an action is morally right when it produces the best overall consequences. There are two basic principles to consequentialism:

1. An act is right or wrong based solely on its results.
2. The more good consequences created from an act, the better and more right that act is.

While consequentialism can provide guidance for how one should live his life (we should live to maximize the amount of good consequences) and how to react during a moral dilemma (we should choose the action that will maximize the good consequences), consequentialism has been met with its fair share of criticism.

In consequentialism, it proves challenging to predict future consequences. How does one go about assessing the morality of a consequence? Should it be based on what an individual believed would happen, or should it be based on what actually happened? There are also issues with how to measure and compare consequences that are morally "good." According to hedonism, a form of consequentialism, good is measured by pleasure, while in utilitarianism, another type of consequentialism, good is measured by well-being and welfare.

In the case of the trolley problem, we begin to see how consequentialism unravels. In the first case, one form of utilitarianism claims pulling the lever is, morally speaking, the better choice. However, another type of utilitarianism claims that since something morally wrong is already happening, participating by pulling the lever would also be morally wrong because you are now partially responsible for the death of a person or persons, whereas before, you were not.

In the case of the second scenario, many people who were willing to pull the lever were not willing to throw the fat man over the bridge. While the consequences in both situations remain the same (you choose to save the five people and one person dies), there seems to exist a moral difference between simply pulling the lever and actually throwing a person over a bridge.

THE DOCTRINE OF DOUBLE EFFECT

The problem of the trolley is based on a principle known as the doctrine of double effect. This principle, first introduced by Thomas Aquinas, is the notion that an action can be morally permissible even when one of the consequences is morally bad. The bad consequence of these actions is foreseen, like in the problem of the trolley, where you realize ahead of time that one man will die if the lever is pulled.

So if harming others is considered immoral, and we can foresee that one of the consequences involves harming another person, is the person who pulls the lever morally wrong?

According to the doctrine of double effect, an individual can morally perform an action that leads to foreseen harmful consequences if the following four conditions are met:

1. **There must be intention for the good consequence.** The good consequence should never be used as an excuse for the bad consequence, so there should never be the intention to have the bad consequence occur.
2. **The action itself must be morally neutral or good, and never morally wrong.** So if you were to isolate the action from the good and bad consequences, it should never be bad.
3. **The good consequence must be the direct result of the action, and not the result of the bad consequence.** A morally good consequence can never occur because the action initially created a bad consequence.
4. **The bad consequence can never outweigh the good consequence.** Even if the intent was good, if the result leads to the bad consequence overpowering the good consequence, then this condition has been violated.

A common real-life example of the doctrine of double effect is when someone is killed out of self-defense. If someone kills his attacker, the action is morally permissible because the good consequence outweighs the foreseen bad consequence (killing another person).

The doctrine of double effect is rejected by consequentialists because according to consequentialism, there is no relevance to what a person intended; only the consequences of his actions matter.

To this day, the questions of morality proposed by the trolley problem continue to spark debate in the philosophical world.

REALISM

The theory of universals

Realism is the philosophical theory that claims universals exist in the world independent of mind and language.

Philosophical Definitions

UNIVERSALS: First introduced by Plato, universals are repeatable and common characteristics that exist in the world and are often divided into two categories—properties (like squareness, for example) and qualities (like similarity). Though few, if any, properties and qualities are shared by everything, realists assert that universals do reveal a genuine commonality in nature and provide a systematized order to the world.

So, according to realism, a red apple and a red cherry have a universal essence of "redness." Realists claim that the property "redness" does, in fact, exist even if there are no minds to perceive it. In this example, the apple and the cherry are particulars. In other words, they are not themselves universals, but are said to represent them.

TYPES OF REALISM

There are many different types of realism that touch on morality, politics, religion, science, and metaphysics. Two of the most well-known forms of realism include:

1. **Extreme Realism:** This is the oldest form of realism, initially created by Plato. To Plato, universals (which he refers to as Forms) are immaterial and exist outside of space and time.
2. **Strong Realism:** This form of realism rejects Plato's idea of Forms, and instead claims that universals not only exist in space and time; they can also exist in many entities at the same time. The redness in the apple and cherry is actually the same universal redness, and not distinct from entity to entity.

Realism attempts to answer the "problem of universals," which is the question of whether or not universals exist in the first place.

OBJECTIONS TO REALISM

Realism is a much-debated subject in philosophy. While there are many objections to realism, these arguments do little to disprove realism entirely, and cannot be used to deny the existence of universals.

Argument from Oddity
Philosopher Bertrand Russell's "argument from oddity" states:

- **Premise 1:** Universals are extremely odd entities (after all, their very nature and existence is strange and hard to identify).
- **Premise 2:** If universals are extremely odd entities, then they don't exist.
- **Premise 3:** If universals don't exist, then realism is false.
- Therefore, realism is false.

In *The Problems of Philosophy*, Russell describes a relation between two places: "Edinburgh is north of London." This relation seems to exist independently of human perception. Russell asserts, however, that there are objections against this conclusion; antirealists (those who subscribe to the belief that there is nothing outside of the mind and even if there were, we would not be able to access it) claim that universals do not exist in the same sense as physical objects or particulars.

While it is easy to say where and when London exists (on a specific part of the earth, from the time it was created until the time it is destroyed), it is impossible to say the same of the relation "north of" because that entity does not exist in time or space. Therefore, as stated by the first premise of the argument, it is rational to believe that universals are very strange entities. The argument goes on to say that because universals are odd in that they do not exist in any spatiotemporal sense, it follows that universals do not exist at all (Premise 2). Because it is impossible to know when or where a universal is, it is logical to deny its existence. If universals do not exist, then the theory that claims they do exist, realism, is false (Premise 3). Premise 3 is the negation of realism.

Because the "argument from oddity" is a valid argument, it seems at first to be a solid objection to realism. Further analysis of its definition of existence, however, demonstrates the argument to be far less sound. The main problem with the argument is its leap from the first premise to the second. Though universals may indeed be odd in that they don't exist in a spatiotemporal realm, it does not mean that they do not exist at all. It may seem rational to view spatiotemporal existence as the only type of existence, but this is not the case. Indeed, while physical objects, thoughts, emotions, etc., exist, universals can be said to subsist. Universals subsist rather than exist (meaning they exist without space or time), says Russell, because they are timeless and unchangeable. Ultimately, though universals exist in an odd way, they do, indeed, exist.

Problem of Individuation

A second objection to realism is called the "problem of individuation." This objection states:

- **Premise 1:** If realism is true, then there are universals.
- **Premise 2:** If there are universals, then it is possible to individuate universals.
- **Premise 3:** It is not possible to individuate universals.
- Therefore, realism is not true.

To *individuate* a universal means to know of a "criterion of identity" for that universal. In other words, to individuate a universal means to know a necessarily true, noncircular statement of the form.

The first premise simply states the theory of realism. Premise 2 asserts that if universals exist, then it must be possible to know their form (in the same way one can say, for example, X is the same event as Y if and only if X and Y share the same cause and effect). When attempting to individuate a universal, the result becomes a circular argument, therefore proving Premise 3 to be true.

Like the "argument from oddity," the "problem of individuation" is a valid but unsound argument. It may very well be the case that universals can, indeed, be individuated, but we have not yet determined a way to articulate their form. Unless the "problem of individuation" can prove that universals absolutely cannot be individuated at any point in the future, rather than simply stating that they have not been individuated in the past, the argument has no logical merit.

IMMANUEL KANT (1724–1804)

Human reason and modern thought

Immanuel Kant is one of the single most important philosophers to have ever lived. His work forever changed the shape of Western philosophy. Born on April 22, 1724, in Königsberg, East Prussia, Kant came from a large and modest family. As Kant grew older, the popular Protestant movement Pietism played a large role in his family's life (and would subsequently influence his later work).

At eight years old, Kant attended the Collegium Fridericianum, where he studied classicism. Kant remained there until 1740, when he enrolled in the University of Königsberg, studying mathematics and philosophy. When his father died in 1746, Kant found himself suddenly without money and began to take work as a private tutor to pay for his education. He worked as a tutor for seven years, and it was during this time that Kant published many of his philosophical ideas.

Kant worked as a lecturer at the University of Königsberg for fifteen years, until finally, in 1770, he became a professor in logic and metaphysics. When he was fifty-seven years old, Kant published the *Critique of Pure Reason*, which is one of the single most important philosophical texts ever written. In his book, Kant detailed how the human mind organizes experiences in two ways: how the world appears, and how one thinks about the world.

Kant continued to teach at the University of Königsberg and write major philosophical texts for the next twenty-seven years. However, as word spread of his unorthodox methods of teaching religious texts, the Prussian government began to pressure Kant. In 1792, the king of Prussia barred Immanuel Kant from writing about and teaching religious subjects, which Kant obeyed until the king's death five years later.

Kant taught at the same school until his retirement in 1796. Though his life was relatively ordinary, his contributions to philosophy were anything but.

THE CRITIQUES OF IMMANUEL KANT

The work of Immanuel Kant is immense and incredibly complex. However, the common theme throughout all of his work is his use of a critical method to understand and come to terms with philosophical problems. Kant believed that in philosophy, one should not speculate about the world around him; rather, we should all critique our own mental abilities. We should investigate all that we are familiar with, understand and define the limits of our knowledge, and determine how our mental processes affect how we make sense of everything. Rather than speculating on the universe around us, Kant believed that by looking inward we would discover the answers to the many questions posed by philosophy. Thus, Kant shifts away from metaphysics and toward epistemology (the study of knowledge).

Transcendental Idealism
To understand Kant's philosophy of transcendental idealism, one must first understand Kant's distinction between phenomena and noumena.

Philosophical Definitions

PHENOMENA: According to Kant, phenomena are the realities or appearances that are interpreted from our minds. **NOUMENA:** These, according to Kant, are the things that exist regardless of our minds' interpretations.

Kant claims that we only have the ability to know the world that is presented to us from our minds and that the external world can never truly be known. In other words, the only knowledge that we know, and ever will know, is knowledge of phenomena. This means that knowledge of noumena is, and always will be, unknown.

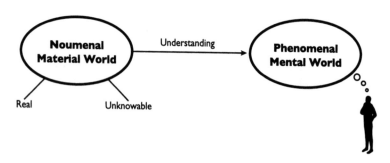

In philosophy, *idealism* refers to the various notions that share the belief that the world is composed not of physical things, but of mental ideas. In Kant's transcendental idealism, however, Kant does not deny that an external reality exists. Nor does he assume that things are less fundamental than ideas. Instead, Kant claims that our minds contextualize and limit reality, and that we will never be able to transcend these limitations.

The Synthetic *A Priori*

Kant attempts to answer the question of how, when the nature of experience is individual and particular (for example, we each experience sights and sounds individually), there can be universal truths from experience. How can we infer cause and effect when we cannot experience (see, smell, touch, etc.) the law of causation?

Kant makes a distinction between two types of propositions:

1. **Analytic proposition:** This is when the concept is contained within the subject. For example, "all squares have four corners." In this sentence, four corners is part of the definition of a square.
2. **Synthetic proposition:** This is when the concept is not contained within the subject. For example, "all women are happy." In this sentence, happiness is not part of the definition of a woman.

Kant then makes a distinction between two more propositions:

1. *a priori* **proposition:** This is when the justification of a proposition does not rely on any experience. For example, "8 + 6 = 14" or "all mice are rodents."
2. *a posteriori* **proposition:** This is when the justification of a proposition relies on experience. For example, the proposition "all women are happy" requires experience to say whether or not it is true.

Kant asks how synthetic *a priori* knowledge can be possible (in other words, how one can know something is universal and necessary without it being definitional or self-evident). Kant concludes that synthetic *a priori* knowledge is in fact possible. And here's how:

According to Kant, experience is organized in our mind based on certain categories. These categories then become features of experience that are both necessary and universal. For example, it is not that we can't find causation in nature. Rather, causation is a feature in our minds, so we always perceive it. We can't *not* find causation. The synthetic *a priori*, according to Kant, is how people develop substantive knowledge.

KANT'S VIEWS ON ETHICS

Kant was a deontologist, meaning he firmly believed that an action should be determined as moral or immoral based on the motive behind the action (as opposed to consequentialists, who judge an action's morality based on its consequences). According to Kant, since we have the ability to deliberate and provide reasons for an action, moral judgment should be placed on those reasons why an action was performed. While it is important that our actions have good consequences and we should always try for that result, consequences are not affected by reason, and therefore, reason is not completely responsible for the consequences of a particular action that was endorsed by reason.

Reason can only be held accountable for endorsing a particular action. Therefore, we can only judge motives and actions as being moral or immoral. Since morality is determined from reason, this means that goodness and badness also stem from reason.

Kant claims that acting badly is violating the maxims created from one's own personal reason, or creating maxims that cannot consistently be viewed as universal laws. In other words, badness is the result of laws of reason being violated. From this notion, we can conclude that immorality is actually a type of irrationality because the laws of reason are being violated. By acting immorally, Kant believes that we become less rational human beings, thus weakening our humanity. We can only stop ourselves from doing things against our better judgment by behaving rationally.

DUALISM

The mind and the body separated

Dualism attempts to answer the mind-body problem, which asks what the relationship is between an individual's physical properties and an individual's mental properties.

According to dualism, the mind and body are two separate things. While the body (or matter) is the physical substance that an individual is made of, the mind (or soul) is a nonphysical substance that exists apart from the body and includes consciousness.

There are three major types of dualism:

1. **Substance Dualism:** Substance can be broken down into two categories: mental and material. According to René Descartes, who made this theory famous, the material substance does not have the ability to think, and the mental substance has no extension in the physical world.

2. **Property Dualism:** The mind and body exist as properties of one material substance. In other words, consciousness is the result of matter being organized in a specific way (like the human brain).

3. **Predicate Dualism:** In order to make sense of the world, there needs to be more than one predicate (the way we go about describing a proposition's subject). According to predicate dualism, mental predicates cannot be reduced into physical predicates. For example, in the sentence "Troy is annoying," one cannot reduce the act of "being annoying" into a physical thing (predicate). "Annoying" cannot be defined by its structure or composition, and it can look different in different situations.

The Brain

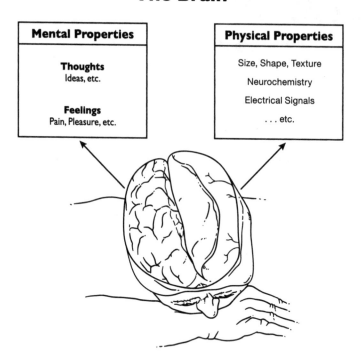

Mental Properties	Physical Properties
Thoughts Ideas, etc. **Feelings** Pain, Pleasure, etc.	Size, Shape, Texture Neurochemistry Electrical Signals . . . etc.

ARGUMENTS FOR DUALISM

There are several arguments that support the claims of dualism. In particular, dualism is very popular among those who believe in the existence of a soul that is separate from one's physical body.

The Subjective Argument

One of the more famous arguments supporting substance dualism is the subjective argument. This argues that mental events feature subjective qualities, while physical events do not. For a mental event, one can ask questions about what something looks, feels, or sounds like. However, those sensations cannot be reduced into a physical event. Even though you can see, touch, or hear physical events, when you are describing a sensation such as "what something feels like," you cannot actually reduce it to something physical. It is still a sensation with subjective qualities.

The Special Sciences Argument

The special sciences argument supports the notion of predicate dualism. If predicate dualism is true, then "special sciences" must exist. These sciences should not be able to be reduced any further using the laws of physics. Because psychology, which cannot be further reduced by the laws of physics, exists as a form of science, this must imply that the mind exists. Even the science of meteorology proves the special science argument to be true, because studying weather patterns is only of interest to people, and therefore, this science presupposes that the mind cares and is interested in weather. Therefore, in order for the material world to be perceived mentally, there must be a perspective from the mind about the material world.

Argument from Reason

According to the argument from reason, if our thoughts are simply the result of physical causes, then there is no reason to believe that these thoughts are based on reason or are rational. A physical material is not rational, and yet we as humans have reason. Therefore, the mind must not simply be from a material source.

ARGUMENTS AGAINST DUALISM

There are many arguments against dualism. Many of these arguments fall under a broader belief known as monism, which states that instead of two separate substances, the mind and body are part of one substance.

Monism in a Nutshell

- **Idealistic Monism (also known as Idealism):** The only substance that exists is the mental substance (consciousness).
- **Materialistic Monism (also known as Physicalism):** The physical world is the only reality, and anything mental stems from the physical.
- **Neutral Monism:** There exists one substance that is neither physical nor mental, but is where physical and mental attributes come from.

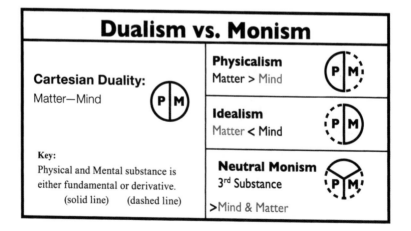

Argument from Brain Damage

This argument against dualism questions how the theory works when, for example, brain damage from trauma to the head, pathological diseases, or drug abuse leads to a compromised mental ability. If the mental and the material truly were separate from one another, the mental should be unaffected by such events. In fact, scientists have discovered that there is most likely a causal relationship between the mind and the brain, and that by manipulating or damaging the brain, mental states are affected.

Causal Interaction

The argument of causal interaction questions how something immaterial (the mental) has the ability to affect the material. It is still very unclear where such interactions would occur. If you were to burn your finger, for example, a chain of events would unfold. First, the skin is burned; then nerve endings become stimulated. Eventually, the peripheral nerves lead to a specific part of the brain, and the result is the feeling of pain. However, if dualism were true, pain would not be able to be located in a particular spot. However, the pain *is* located in a particular spot, the finger.

Additionally, the theory of causal interaction deals with how an interaction occurs between the mental and the physical. Let's say you move your arm up and down. To do so, you first have the intention to move your arm up and down (the mental event). The message travels via neurons, and then you move your arm up and down. However, the mental event of intending to move your arm is not enough to move your arm. There must be a force that makes the neurons send the message. Dualism lacks the explanation of how a nonphysical event can create a physical event.

Argument from Simplicity

Perhaps the most common argument against dualism is also the simplest. The argument from simplicity ponders why someone would attempt to explain the existence of the mind and body in two parts when doing so in one part is simpler.

This is expressed through the principle known as "Occam's razor," which states that, when explaining a phenomenon, one shouldn't multiply entities beyond what is necessary. Therefore, it should be rational for humans to want the simplest explanation.

While parts of dualism have their strengths, there is no denying that dualism does not answer all of the questions that arise from the mind-body problem.

UTILITARIANISM

Measuring happiness

In analyzing moral behavior, two questions are often raised:

1. What makes an act right or wrong?
2. Which things are good, and which are bad?

Utilitarianism, introduced by Jeremy Bentham and later altered by John Stuart Mill, is the most common consequentialist theory. It holds that the only thing of value, and the only thing that is good in itself, is happiness. Though other things have value, their value is merely derived from their contribution to happiness.

JEREMY BENTHAM (1748–1832)

English philosopher Jeremy Bentham, influenced by the work of Hume and Hobbes, introduced the foundation of utilitarianism in his 1789 book, *Introduction to the Principles of Morals and Legislation*. In his book, Bentham created the principle of utility, in which an action is approved of when it has the tendency to provide and enable the most happiness.

According to Bentham, happiness is defined as the presence of pleasure and the absence of pain. He created a formula, known as the felicific (meaning "happiness-making") calculus, with which to measure the value of different pleasures and pains. When measuring pleasure and pain, Bentham looks at duration, intensity, certainty versus uncertainty, and nearness versus farness. Bentham then reasons that what makes an act right is the extent to which it increases the pleasure and decreases the pain. His theory is identified as hedonistic because it believes pleasure and pain to be the only things of value and is referred to as "act utilitarianism" because it applies utility directly to actions.

For Bentham, utilitarianism was based on the consequences of actions that were taken. Most importantly, Bentham emphasized the happiness of the community as the most important thing, since the happiness of the community is the sum of the happiness of the individual people within the community. Therefore, the principle of utility determined that the moral obligation to perform an action was based on doing whatever produced the greatest amount of happiness in the largest number of people affected by the action. For Bentham, it was about quantity over quality. No matter how complex or simple the pleasure, each was treated the same. Bentham firmly believed more, quantitatively speaking, is better.

Bentham's Views on Crime

Bentham believed social policies should be evaluated based on the general well-being of those affected, and that punishing criminals effectively discouraged crime because it made individuals compare the benefits of committing a crime to the pain involved in the punishment.

JOHN STUART MILL (1806–1873)

John Stuart Mill, an admirer and follower of Bentham's, extended and altered the theories of Jeremy Bentham in his 1861 book, *Utilitarianism*.

While Mill agreed with and enhanced much of Bentham's theory, he disagreed with the belief that quantity of pleasure is better than quality. Mill noted that, with Bentham's disregard for qualitative differences, there was no difference between the value of a human's pleasure and the value of an animal's pleasure. Thus, the moral status of humans is the same as the moral status of animals.

While Mill believed that pleasures differed in quality, he proved that quality could not be quantified (thus showing that Bentham's felicific calculus was unreasonable). To Mill, only those people who had experienced high pleasures and low pleasures would be able to judge their quality, and this process would lead to the creation of a moral worth that would promote higher pleasures (which he believed were mostly intellectual), even if the lower pleasures (which he believed were mostly bodily) were momentarily more intense.

According to Mill, happiness is difficult to attain. Thus, instead of seeking pleasure, people are morally justified to instead seek out a way to reduce their total amount of pain with their actions. Mill's form of utilitarianism also allowed for the ability to sacrifice pleasure and experience pain if the result is for the greater good of everyone.

Mill responds to critics who claim that utilitarianism asks too much of people by explaining that most good actions are not intended for the world's benefit, but for the benefit of individuals who make up the world. This private utility is what most people attend to, and it is rare that any person has the power to be a public benefactor.

TYPES OF UTILITARIANISM

While there are many types of utilitarianism, the two most well-known forms are act utilitarianism and rule utilitarianism.

Act Utilitarianism

In act utilitarianism, only the results and consequences of a single act are taken into account, and an act is deemed morally right when it creates the best (or less bad) results for the largest number of people. Act utilitarianism looks at each individual act and calculates utility each time the act is performed. Morality is then determined by how useful the results are to the largest amount of people affected.

However, act utilitarianism has its criticisms. Not only can it prove challenging under act utilitarianism to have a complete knowledge of the consequences of one's actions; the principle also allows for immoral acts to be justified. For example, if there is a war between two countries and the war can end by finding the whereabouts of one man who is in hiding, act utilitarianism states that torturing the man's child, who knows of his father's location, would be morally justified.

Rule Utilitarianism

While act utilitarianism looks at the results of a single act, rule utilitarianism measures the results of an act as it is repeated through time, as if it were a rule. According to rule utilitarianism, an action is considered morally right when it complies with the rules that lead to the greatest overall happiness.

Rule utilitarianism states that an action is morally correct based on the correctness of its rules. When a rule is correct and followed, the result is the greatest amount of good or happiness that can be attained. According to rule utilitarianism, while following the rules may not lead to the greatest overall happiness, not following the rules will not either.

Rule utilitarianism also faces criticism. For example, in rule utilitarianism, it is entirely possible to create rules that are unjust. A perfect real-world example is slavery. Rule utilitarianism could claim that slavery is morally right if the mistreatment of a select group of people results in an overall happiness.

WHAT IS RIGHT OR WRONG?

In both act utilitarianism and rule utilitarianism, nothing is ever simply right or wrong on its own. No matter the type of utilitarianism, neither form appears to require an absolute ban on lying, cheating, or stealing. Indeed, utilitarianism seems at times to require that we lie, cheat, or steal so long as it is the route by which maximum happiness is achieved (though according to rule utilitarianism, activities like lying, cheating, and stealing would undermine the trust upon which human society is founded, and any rule which permits these actions cannot maximize utility if it is universally adopted).

In utilitarianism, morality is always based on the consequences that arise as a result of an action, and never based on the actual action. Because of this focus on consequences rather than intentions, the moral worth of an action seems to become a matter of luck. The final consequences of an action must become evident before it can be determined whether the action was good or bad. However, we can certainly imagine actions with good intentions that ultimately lead to bad consequences, as well as actions with bad intentions that lead to good consequences. Furthermore, because it is necessary to determine how many people will be affected, how intensely they will be affected, and the effect of any available alternatives, utilitarianism leaves much room for miscalculation. Therefore, though utilitarianism does an adequate job of banning deceitful behavior, it seems to be a weak moral theory.

JOHN LOCKE (1632–1704)

The rights of man

John Locke was born on August 29, 1632, in Somerset, England, to a Puritan family. Locke's father, a lawyer who also served as a captain in the English Civil War, was well connected with the English government. As a result, Locke was able to receive an outstanding and diverse education. In 1647, while attending Westminster School in London, Locke was named King's Scholar (an honor bestowed upon only a select few), and in 1652, Locke attended Oxford's most prestigious school, Christ Church. It was at Christ Church that John Locke became familiar with metaphysics and logic, and while pursuing his Master of Arts, he immersed himself in the work of Descartes and Robert Boyle (who is considered to be the father of chemistry) and pursued a career as a doctor.

In 1665, Locke became friends with Lord Ashley (who was a founder of the Whig party and would go on to become Earl of Shaftesbury), one of England's most skilled statesmen, who came to Oxford looking for medical treatment. Lord Ashley invited Locke to live in London and work for him as his personal physician, and Locke moved there in 1667. As Lord Ashley's power and responsibility grew, so too did Locke's responsibilities, and he soon found himself working in trading and colonization. One project Lord Ashley took on was the colonization of the Carolinas in the New World, and Locke took part in writing the constitution for the land. It was during this time that Locke started to become interested in philosophical discussions.

In 1674, with Lord Ashley no longer in government, Locke returned to Oxford to get a bachelor of medicine degree and then traveled to France, where he spent a lot of his time learning about Protestantism. Upon returning to England in 1679, Locke found himself embroiled in controversy. As Charles II and Parliament fought for control and revolution seemed possible, Locke's involvement in a failed assassination attempt of the king and the king's brother forced Locke to leave the country. It was during this time that Locke also wrote the highly regarded *Two Treatises of Government*.

While living in exile in Holland, Locke finished perhaps what is his most famous work, *An Essay Concerning Human Understanding*, which he had started while in France. Locke was finally able to return to England in 1688, when William of Orange invaded England, forcing James II (who ruled after his brother, Charles II, died) to flee to France, starting the Glorious Revolution. It was only after Locke's return to England that *An Essay Concerning Human Understanding* and *Two Treatises of Government* were published.

The Glorious Revolution had a profound impact on England and shifted power away from the monarchy and toward Parliament. John Locke was not only considered to be a hero during his time; his contributions to Western philosophy have proven that he is one of the greatest minds of human history. His philosophical works touched on empiricism, epistemology, government, God, religious toleration, and private property.

AN ESSAY CONCERNING HUMAN UNDERSTANDING

John Locke's most famous work, *An Essay Concerning Human Understanding*, deals with fundamental questions regarding the mind, thought, language, and perception, and is broken up into four books. In *Essay*, Locke provides a systematic philosophy that attempts to answer the question of how we think. As a result of his work, Locke shifted the philosophical dialogue away from metaphysics and toward epistemology.

Locke opposes the notion set forth by other philosophical schools (such as those of Plato and Descartes) that one is born with innate, fundamental principles and knowledge. He argues that this idea would mean all humans universally accept certain principles, and since there are no universally accepted principles (and if there were, they would not be the result of innate knowledge), this cannot be true.

For example, people differ in moral ideas, so moral knowledge cannot be innate. Instead, Locke believed that humans are a *tabula rasa*, or blank slate, that gain knowledge through experience. The experience creates simple ideas (based on the senses, reflection, and sensation), and as these simple ideas combine, they become more complex (through comparison, abstraction, and combination) and form knowledge. Ideas can also be divided into two categories:

1. **Primary** (which cannot be separate from the matter and are present regardless of whether a person sees them or not—for example, size, shape, and motion)
2. **Secondary** (which are separate from the matter and are only perceived when the matter is observed—for example, taste and odor)

Lastly, Locke objects to Plato's concept of essences, the notion that humans can only identify an individual to be part of a species because of its essence. Locke creates his own theory of essences based on observable properties (which he calls nominal essences) and the invisible structures that form the observable properties (which he calls real essences). For example, we can form an idea and create an essence about what a dog is based on what we observe and based on the biology of the dog (which is responsible for the observable properties). To Locke, human knowledge is limited, and humans should be aware of such limitations.

TWO TREATISES OF GOVERNMENT

In his *Two Treatises of Government*, Locke details his beliefs on human nature and politics. The anchor to Locke's political philosophy was the notion that humans have the right to private property.

According to Locke, when God created man, man only had to live by the laws of nature, and as long as peace was preserved, one could do as he pleased. Man's right to self-preservation meant that man also had the right to have the things that are needed in order for one to survive and live happily; and those have been provided by God.

Since man is the owner of his own body, any product or good that is the result of his physical labor should also belong to him. A man who decides to farm and create food, for example, should therefore be the owner of that land and the food produced from the land. According to Locke's ideas on private property, one should not take possession of something if another individual is harmed in the process because God wants everyone to be happy, and man should not take more than he needs, for that could be used by another person. Since immoral people exist, however, man should create laws to ensure and protect his rights to property and freedoms.

It is the sole purpose of government, Locke believed, to support the well-being of everyone. And though some natural rights are surrendered when a government is established, a government has the ability to protect rights more effectively than one person could alone. If the government no longer supports the well-being of everyone, it should be replaced, and it is the moral obligation of the community to revolt.

According to Locke, if a proper government exists, both individuals and societies should flourish not only materially, but spiritually. The government should provide a freedom that aligns with the self-perpetuating natural law created by God.

Though published later in his life, once Locke had returned to England after living in exile, *Two Treatises of Government* was written during a time of great political tension between the monarchy and Parliament. Locke believed that there could be a greater type of government, and his political philosophy had a profound impact on Western philosophy.

EMPIRICISM VERSUS RATIONALISM

Where do truths come from?

In epistemology, philosophers examine the nature, origins, and limits of knowledge. The questions raised in epistemology are:

- How can one gain knowledge?
- What are the limits of knowledge?
- What is the nature of true knowledge? What warrants it to be true?

In answering the first question about how knowledge originates, there are two contrasting theories in philosophy: empiricism and rationalism.

EMPIRICISM

Empiricism is the theory that all knowledge comes from sensory experience. According to empiricism, our senses obtain the raw information from the world around us, and our perception of this raw information starts a process whereby we begin to formulate ideas and beliefs. The notion that humans are born with an innate knowledge is rejected, and it is argued that humans only have knowledge that is *a posteriori*, meaning "based on experience." Through inductive reasoning of the basic observations provided by the senses, knowledge becomes more complex.

In general, there are three types of empiricism:

Classical Empiricism

This is the form of empiricism associated with John Locke's *tabula rasa* theory. The notion of an innate knowledge is completely rejected, and it is assumed that we know nothing at birth. It is only as one begins to experience the world that information is gathered and knowledge is formed.

Radical Empiricism

Radical empiricism was made famous by American philosopher William James. In the most radical forms of empiricism, all of one's knowledge comes from the senses. One would then be able to conclude from this that the meaning of a statement is connected to experiences that are able to confirm that statement. This is known as the verificationist principle, and it is part of a type of radical empiricism known as logical positivism (which has become an unpopular form of empiricism). Because all knowledge comes from the senses, according to logical positivism, it is not possible to talk about something that has not been experienced. If a statement cannot be linked to experience, that statement is meaningless. For logical positivism to be true, religious and ethical beliefs would have to be abandoned because there are no experiences or observations one could have that would be able to confirm such claims, making them meaningless.

Moderate Empiricism

This form of empiricism, which seems more plausible than radical empiricism, allows for cases where knowledge is not grounded in the senses (though these are still known as exceptions to the rule). For example, in "9 + 4 = 13" we see a truth that does not require investigation. However, any significant forms of knowledge are still solely gained from experience.

RATIONALISM

Rationalism is the theory that reason, not the senses, is where knowledge originates. Rationalists claim that without having principles
and categories already in place, humans would not be able to orga-
nize or interpret the information provided by the senses. Therefore,
according to rationalism, humans must have innate concepts and
then use deductive reasoning.

Rationalists believe in at least one of the following:

The Intuition/Deduction Thesis

This thesis states that there are some propositions that are
known as a result of intuition alone, while other propositions can be
known by being deduced from an intuited proposition. According to
rationalism, intuition is a type of rational insight. Through deduction,
we are able to arrive at conclusions from intuited premises by using
valid arguments. In other words, the conclusion has to be true if
the premises on which the conclusion is based are true. Once one
piece of knowledge is known, one can then deduce others from that
original knowledge.

For example, one can intuit that the number 5 is a prime number and
less than 6, and then one can deduce that there is a prime number that is
less than 6. Any knowledge that is gained from the intuition/deduction
thesis is *a priori*, meaning it has been gained independent of the senses,
and rationalists have used it to explain mathematics, ethics, free will,
and even metaphysical claims like the existence of God.

The Innate Knowledge Thesis

This thesis states that, as part of our rational nature, we have
knowledge of some truths within a particular subject. Like the

intuition/deduction thesis, the innate knowledge thesis states that knowledge is acquired *a priori*. According to this thesis, however, knowledge does not come from intuition or deduction; rather, it is just part of our very nature to have it. The source of the knowledge depends upon the philosopher. While some rationalists believe this knowledge comes from God, for example, others believe it to be the result of natural selection.

The Innate Concept Thesis

This theory states that as part of our nature, humans have concepts that they employ in a specific subject. According to the innate concept thesis, some knowledge is not the result of experience; however, sensory experience can trigger the process that brings this knowledge to our consciousness. While experience can act as a trigger, it still does not provide concepts or determine what the information is. This concept is different from the innate knowledge thesis because here, knowledge can be deduced from innate concepts. With the innate concept thesis, the more removed a concept is from experience, the more plausible it is to claim it as innate. For example, a concept on geometric shapes would be more innate than a concept on experiencing pain because it is further removed from experience.

While empiricism and rationalism present two different explanations for the same question, the answers are sometimes not as black and white. For example, philosophers Gottfried Wilhelm Leibniz and Baruch Spinoza, considered to be key figures in the rationalism movement, believed that knowledge could be gained through reason in principle. However, besides specific areas like mathematics, they did not think it was possible in practice.

GEORG WILHELM FRIEDRICH HEGEL (1770–1831)

The power of others

Georg Wilhelm Friedrich Hegel's father wished for his son to become a clergyman. Hegel enrolled in the seminary at the University of Tübingen in 1788 and studied theology. During his time at the University, Hegel became friends with Friedrich Hölderlin and Friedrich W. J. von Schelling, who would go on to become incredibly successful as a poet and philosopher, respectively. Throughout their lives, these three men would have profound impacts on one another's work.

After graduating, Hegel decided he would not pursue being a pastor and lived in Frankfurt, where he worked as a tutor. When his father died, Hegel was left with enough money to financially support himself and began to devote his time entirely to working on his religious and social philosophies. In 1800, Hegel was introduced to the work of Immanuel Kant and became very interested in Kant's philosophies. In 1801, Hegel moved with von Schelling to the city of Jena, where both were hired to teach at the University of Jena. Jena was an artistic and intellectual epicenter, and Hegel decided his philosophy would combine his influences of theology, Kantian idealism, and romanticism with contemporary politics and social issues. That same year, Hegel began publishing his philosophical texts.

Hegel published one of his most famous works, *Phenomenology of Spirit*, in 1807, in which he discussed in depth his views on Spirit, consciousness, and knowledge. Hegel would later systematize his philosophical approach in his three-volume *Encyclopedia of the Philosophical Sciences* of 1817 and, in 1821, his *Elements of the*

Philosophy of Right, where he combined his philosophical ideas with critiques of modern society and political institutions.

In the years leading up to his death, Hegel became quite influential. The impact of Georg Wilhelm Friedrich Hegel can be seen in theology, cultural theory, and sociology, and his work is often considered a precursor to Marxism.

DIALECTIC AND SPIRIT

Prior to Hegel's work, the word *dialectic* was used to describe the process of arguing and refuting in order to determine the first principles (like the dialogues made famous by Socrates). Hegel, however, used the word *dialectic* in a very different way.

Like Kant, Hegel was an idealist. Hegel believed the mind only has access to ideas of what the world is like, and that we can never fully perceive what the world is. However, unlike Kant, Hegel believed these ideas were social, meaning they are completely shaped by other people's ideas. Through the use of a common language, traditions of one's society, and the religious and cultural institutions that one belongs to, an individual's mind is shaped. This collective consciousness of a society, which Hegel refers to as "Spirit," is responsible for shaping one's consciousness and ideas.

Hegel, unlike Kant, believed that this Spirit is constantly evolving. According to Hegel, the spirit evolves by the same kind of pattern as an idea would during an argument, the dialectic. First, there is an idea about the world (much like a thesis), which has an inherent flaw, giving rise to the antithesis. The thesis and antithesis eventually reconcile by creating a synthesis, and a new idea arises comprised of elements of both the thesis and the antithesis.

To Hegel, society and culture follow this pattern, and one could understand all of human history, without the use of logic or empirical data, simply by using logic.

The Dialectic

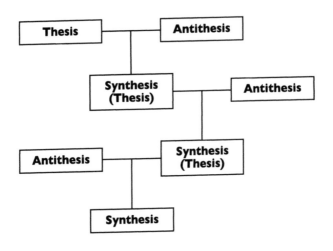

SOCIAL RELATIONS

Hegel agreed with Kant's notion that being conscious of an object also implies one is being self-conscious (because to be conscious of an object means there is also a consciousness of a subject, which would be oneself perceiving the object). Hegel adds to this theory by stating that self-consciousness not only involves an object and a subject; it also involves other subjects because individuals truly become aware of themselves when someone else is watching. Therefore, according to Hegel, actual self-consciousness is social. It is only when another consciousness is present that one views the world from another's eyes in order to get a self-image.

Hegel likens this to relationships of inequality and dependence, where the subordinate in the relationship (known as the bondsman) is consciously aware of his status, while the independent partner (known as the lord) is able to enjoy the freedom of not being concerned about the bondsman's consciousness. However, this creates feelings of guilt for the lord because in order to have this superiority, he must deny the bondsman mutual identification. According to Hegel, this dynamic—where one competes for objectification and mutual identification, and also distances oneself and identifies with another person—is the basis of social life.

ETHICAL LIFE

Hegel describes one cultural expression of Spirit as "ethical life." Ethical life is defined as a reflection of the basic interdependence among people in a society. Hegel lived during the Enlightenment, and as a result, he argued that the tendency of modern life was shifting away from recognizing the essential social bonds. Prior to the Enlightenment, people were regarded by their social hierarchies. However, the Enlightenment, and its key players like Locke, Rousseau, Kant, and Hobbes, placed emphasis on the individual.

Hegel believed the modern state would correct the imbalance set forth by modern culture, and believed institutions were needed that would be able to preserve freedom while affirming ethical life and common bonds. For example, Hegel believed it was the state's job to provide for the poor, regulate the economy, and create institutions based on different occupations (almost like present-day trade unions) so that people can experience a sense of social belonging and a connectivity to a society at large.

RENÉ DESCARTES (1596–1650)

"I think; therefore I am"

René Descartes is considered by many to be the father of modern philosophy. He was born in 1596 in the small French town of La Haye, and his mother died during his first year. His father was an aristocrat who placed great importance on giving his children a good education. At eight years old, Descartes was sent to a Jesuit boarding school, where he would become familiar with logic, rhetoric, metaphysics, astronomy, music, ethics, and natural philosophy.

At twenty-two years old, Descartes earned his law degree from the University of Poitiers (where some believe he had a nervous breakdown) and began studying theology and medicine. He did not pursue them long, however, claiming he wanted to discover the knowledge that was found within himself or the world. He enlisted in the army, where he travelled and, in his spare time, studied mathematics. Descartes ended up becoming acquainted with famous philosopher and mathematician Isaac Beeckman, who was trying to create a method that could link physics and mathematics.

On the night of November 10, 1619, Descartes had three dreams, or visions, that would change the course of his life and philosophy. From these complex dreams, Descartes decided he would devote his life to reforming knowledge through mathematics and science. He began with philosophy because it was the root of all other sciences.

Descartes then began writing *Rules for the Direction of the Mind*, which outlined his new method of thought. The treatise was never finished—Descartes only completed the first of three sections (each composed of twelve rules). It was published posthumously in 1684.

Discourse on the Method

In his first and most famous work, *Discourse on the Method*, Descartes discusses the first set of rules that he created in *Rules for the Direction of the Mind* and how his visions made him doubt everything he knew. He then shows how his rules could solve profound and complex problems, like the existence of God, dualism, and personal existence (where, "I think; therefore I am," comes from).

As Descartes continued to write, his fame grew. Descartes's *Meditations on First Philosophy*, published in 1641, tackled the objections of those who disputed his findings in *Discourse* and introduced a circular form of logic known as a "Cartesian circle." His *Principles of Philosophy*, published in 1644 and read throughout Europe, attempted to find the mathematical foundation of the universe.

While living in Stockholm, Sweden, to tutor the queen, Descartes died from pneumonia. Though he was a devoted Catholic, his work clashed with the church's ideology, and after his death, his books were put on the Catholic Church's index of Prohibited Books.

THE PHILOSOPHICAL THEMES OF RENÉ DESCARTES

Thought and Reason

Descartes is most famous for his statement "Cogito ergo sum," translated as "I think; therefore I am." According to Descartes, the act of thinking is proof of individual existence. Descartes argues that thought and reason are the essence of humanity because while one cannot be sure of any other part of existence, one can always be certain that he has thoughts and reason. For thoughts to exist, there must be a source to do the thinking; therefore if one thinks, one has to exist. To Descartes, humans are also capable of reason, and without it, one would simply not be human.

Descartes believed that it is through the ability to reason that humans gain true knowledge and certainty in science. His assumption that reason is a natural talent gifted to all people led him to write about very complex and philosophical matters in a way that could be understood by all. He even sometimes wrote his works in French instead of Latin (the language used by scholars) so his work could be read by the masses.

Descartes presented arguments as logical trains of thought that anyone would be able to follow. He believed that any problem could be broken up into its simplest parts and that problems could be conveyed as abstract equations. By doing so, one is able to remove the issue of sensory perception (which, according to Descartes, is unreliable) and allow for objective reason to solve the problem.

Since sensory perception was unreliable, the only thing Descartes could truly be sure of was that people are thinking things. Therefore, reason and thought are the essence of all people. And since there is a difference between pure reason and sensory perception, Descartes argues, there must be the existence of the soul.

The Existence of God

Once he was able to establish that man exists solely as a thinking thing, Descartes began to look for other self-evident truths. Descartes concluded that perception and imagination have to exist because they are "modes of consciousness" within the mind, but do not necessarily hold any truths. Therefore, Descartes concludes that the only way to have knowledge of other things is by having knowledge of God.

According to Descartes, since God is perfect, it is impossible for God to deceive someone. Descartes then claims that though he, himself, is imperfect, the fact that he can conceive of the notion of perfection means perfection must exist; and this perfection is God.

The Mind-Body Problem

Descartes was a famous proponent of substance dualism (also referred to as Cartesian dualism), the idea that the mind and body are separate substances.

Descartes believed the rational mind was in control of the body, but that the body could influence the mind to act irrationally, such as when one performs an act of passion. According to Descartes, the mind and body interact with each other at the pineal gland, which he called "the seat of the soul." According to Descartes, like the soul, the pineal gland is a part of the brain that is unitary (though scientific research now shows that it too is split into two hemispheres), and its location near the ventricles makes it the perfect location to influence the nerves that control the body.

Here is Descartes's illustration of dualism. Sensory organs pass information to the pineal gland in the brain, and this information is then sent to the spirit.

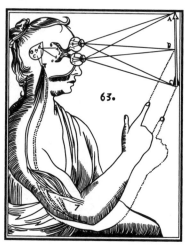

A-THEORY

The past, present, and future

In the philosophical debate over the nature of time, the A-theory is the view held among contemporary philosophers that there exist such intrinsic and indivisible properties as pastness, presentness, and futurity. By virtue of having these A-properties, they claim, events in time are past, present, or future. The origin of this theory is found in *The Unreality of Time*, in which John McTaggart Ellis McTaggart discusses time through what he calls the "A-series" and the "B-series."

THE A-SERIES

According to McTaggart, the A-series is the "series of positions which runs from the far past through the near past to the present, and then from the present through the near future to the far future, or conversely."

By "series of positions," McTaggart means positions in time: Events are positioned in the past if they have already happened; they are positioned in the present if they are happening now; and they are positioned in the future if they have not yet occurred. The property of being in the past, the present, or the future is a temporary, not permanent, property. For example, when it had not yet happened, the event of landing on the moon was in the future; when it was occurring, it was in the present; and now it is in the past.

The "A-series" that McTaggart discusses thus establishes a flow of time, in which each event is at one time future, at one time present, and at one time past, but never any combination of the three at once and never any of the three forever. No event is always present, always past, or always future. His definition also allows for the existence of varying degrees of past and future (next year is, for example, more future than next Tuesday) and different properties that correspond to these different degrees. To talk about events as occurring in either the past, present, or future requires the use of A-sentences, or tensed sentences. An event in the future *will take* place; an event in the present *is taking* place; and an event in the past *has taken* place.

PRESENTISM AND NON-REDUCTIONISM

The A-theory combines presentism and non-reductionism. Presentism is the extreme assertion that only the present is real and that nothing exists other than what presently exists. For example, though past objects, such as dinosaurs, *did* exist, there is no sense in which they *do* exist. Similarly, while it is possible that future objects, such as the 100th president of the United States, *will* exist, it is not the case that they *do* exist. In this context, then, discussion of past or future objects is not a discussion of objects that exist somewhere other than the present, but of properties that did or will exist when other times were or will be present. The strength of presentism depends upon the existence of tenses and is thus an important element of the A-theory.

Non-reductionism, or "taking tense seriously," is the idea that tense corresponds to a fundamental and ineliminable feature of reality. A tensed proposition, or an A-sentence, is one in which tenses (am, was, will, have, had, etc.) are used. An eternal proposition, or a B-sentence, conversely, is a tenseless sentence. Tenseless sentences use words such as *before, after, is simultaneous with,* or specify the date. Non-reductionists claim that tensed propositions cannot be reduced to eternal propositions without a loss of information.

For instance, to say "I believe that I am hungry" does not preserve the same truth value if a date—"I believe that I am hungry at 3 P.M. on June 15"—is attached. A sincere statement of "I believe that I am hungry" entails "I believe that I am hungry simultaneously with my utterance," whereas my statement of "I believe that I am hungry at 3 P.M. on June 15" does not. The A-sentence is true only when it is simultaneous with my saying it. The tenseless sentence, if true, is true at every point in time. This reveals that tensed propositions (A-sentences) convey temporal beliefs that cannot be expressed by tenseless dated sentences.

INCOMPATIBILITY OF THE A-THEORY WITH EINSTEIN'S SPECIAL THEORY OF RELATIVITY

Despite the pervasiveness of tensed sentences in the English language, many philosophers have argued that the A-theory of time is incompatible with special relativity and is thus invalid. Albert Einstein's special theory of relativity (1905) consists of two postulates:

1. The speed of light is the same for all observers, no matter their relative speed.
2. The speed of light is the same in all inertial frames.

It follows from these two postulates that simultaneity is not absolute but must, instead, be relativized to an inertial frame. For any pair of events, there can be no single fact of the matter as to which event happened first, or whether both occurred at the same time. The precedence of one event to the other depends upon the frame of reference: Relative to one frame of reference, Event 1 might be simultaneous with Event 2; relative to another frame of reference, Event 1 might occur earlier than Event 2; and relative to a third frame of reference, Event 1 might occur later than Event 2.

So, while two events might occur simultaneously for one observer, they will occur at different times for an observer moving in a different inertial frame. An event that is present relative to one frame of reference may well be past or future relative to another frame of reference. Because there are no grounds for selecting any single frame of reference as the "real" frame of reference, there can be no absolute, frame-independent distinction between past, present, and future.

RAILWAY EMBANKMENT EXAMPLE

The relativity of simultaneity is found in Einstein's description of an event occurring on a railway embankment: A long train travels at a constant velocity as depicted in the following picture. A person traveling on the train regards all events in reference to the train. Two strokes of lightning occur, one at point A and one at point B. The distance between point A and point B is measured, and an observer is placed at the midpoint, M. The observer is given two mirrors inclined at 90° so that he can observe point A and point B at the same time. If the observer sees the two flashes of light at the same time, the two strokes of lightning are simultaneous. The passenger, however, will see the light from B earlier than from A. Events that are simultaneous with reference to the embankment, then, are not simultaneous with reference to the train.

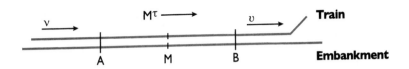

As shown in this example, the absence of an absolute simultaneity poses a problem for the A-theory and the use of tenses. If the special theory of relativity is correct, existence according to presentism becomes a frame-dependent matter. According to two different frames of reference, a single event both exists and does not exist.

ATTEMPTED RECONCILIATION WITH SPECIAL RELATIVITY

Some A-theorists have attempted to reconcile the A-theory with the special theory of relativity. Though the special theory of relativity is well confirmed, these philosophers argue, it remains an empirical theory and should not be used to assess metaphysical claims. In this sense, current physics does not completely *rule out* absolute simultaneity; it just cannot currently conceive of it. An "ideal" physics could detect this currently "unobservable" absolute simultaneity.

Alternatively, A-theorists argue, an absolute simultaneity might never be detectable by physics. The undetectability of absolute simultaneity, however, does not preclude its existence. A final objection posed by A-theorists is that the relativity of simultaneity is itself only an apparent effect. Whether two events are observed simultaneously is one thing; whether they *take place* simultaneously is another.

THE LIAR PARADOX

The contradictions of language

One of the most famous paradoxes in philosophy that is still widely discussed to this day comes from the ancient Greek philosopher Eubulides of Miletus, from the fourth century B.C.

Eubulides of Miletus states the following:

"A man says that he is lying. Is what he says true or false?"

No matter how one answers this question, problems arise because the result is always a contradiction.

If we say the man is telling the truth, that would mean that he is lying, which would then mean that the statement is false.

If we say the man's statement is false, that would mean that he is not lying, and therefore what he says is true.

However, it is not possible to have a statement be both true and false.

EXPLAINING THE LIAR PARADOX

The problem of the liar paradox goes beyond the simple scenario of the lying man that Eubulides portrayed. The liar paradox has very real implications.

Over the years, there have been several philosophers that have theorized about the meaning of the liar paradox. The liar paradox shows that contradictions can arise from common beliefs regarding truth and falsity, and that the notion of truth is a vague one. Furthermore, the liar paradox shows the weakness of language. While the liar paradox is grammatically sound and adheres to the rules of semantics, the sentences produced from the liar paradox have no truth value. Some have even used the liar paradox to prove that the world is incomplete, and therefore there is no such thing as an omniscient being.

To understand the liar paradox, one must first understand the various forms it can take.

The Simple-Falsity Liar

The most basic form of the liar paradox is the simple-falsity liar. This is stated as such:

FLiar: "This sentence is false."

If FLiar is true, then that means "This sentence is false" is true, so therefore FLiar has to be false. FLiar is both true and false, creating a contradiction and a paradox.

If FLiar is false, then that means "This sentence is false" is false, and so FLiar has to be true. FLiar is both false and true, creating a contradiction and a paradox.

The Simple-Untruth Liar

The simple-untruth liar does not work from falsehood, and instead constructs a paradox based on the predicate "not true." The simple-untruth liar appears as:

ULiar: "ULiar is not true."

Like the simple-falsity liar, if ULiar is not true, then it is true; and if it is true, then it is not true. Even if ULiar is neither true nor false, that means it is not true, and since that is precisely what ULiar states, ULiar is true. Thus, another contradiction appears.

LIAR CYCLES

Up until now, we've only seen examples of liar paradoxes that are self-referential. However, even removing the self-referential nature of the paradoxes still creates contradictions. The liar cycles is stated as:

- "The next sentence is true."
- "The previous sentence is not true."

If the first sentence is true, then the second sentence is true, which would make the first sentence not true, thus creating a contradiction. If the first sentence is not true, then the second sentence is not true, which would make the first sentence true, thus creating a contradiction.

POSSIBLE RESOLUTIONS TO THE LIAR PARADOX

The liar paradox has been a source of philosophical debate. Over time, philosophers have created several well-known solutions that allow one to "get out of" the liar paradox.

Arthur Prior's Solution

Philosopher Arthur Prior claimed the liar paradox was not a paradox at all. To Prior, every statement has its own implied assertion of truth. Therefore, a sentence like "This sentence is false" is actually the same as saying, "This sentence is true, and this sentence is false." This creates a simple contradiction, and because you cannot have something be true and false, it has to be false.

Alfred Tarski's Solution

According to philosopher Alfred Tarski, the liar paradox can only arise in a language that is "semantically closed." This refers to any language where there is the ability to have one sentence assert the truth or falsity of itself or another sentence. In order to avoid such contradictions, Tarski believed there should be levels of languages, and that truth or falsity could only be asserted by language that is at a higher level than that sentence. By creating a hierarchy, Tarski was able to avoid self-referential contradictions. Any language that is higher up in the hierarchy may refer to language that is lower; however, not vice versa.

Saul Kripke's Solution

According to Saul Kripke, a sentence is only paradoxical depending on contingent facts. Kripke claimed that when the truth value of a sentence is tied to a fact about the world that can be evaluated, this sentence is "grounded." If the truth value cannot be linked to an evaluable fact about the world, it is "ungrounded," and all ungrounded statements have no truth value. Liar statements and statements similar to liar statements are ungrounded and, therefore, contain no truth value.

Jon Barwise's and John Etchemendy's Solution

To Barwise and Etchemendy, the liar paradox is ambiguous. Barwise and Etchemendy make a distinction between "negation" and "denial." If the liar states, "This sentence is not true," then the liar is negating himself. If the liar states, "It is not the case that this sentence is true," then the liar is denying himself. According to Barwise and Etchemendy, the liar that negates himself can be false without contradiction, and the liar that denies himself can be true without any contradiction.

Graham Priest's Solution

Philosopher Graham Priest is a proponent of dialetheism, the notion that there are true contradictions. A true contradiction is one that is simultaneously true and false. In believing this to be the case, dialetheism must reject the well-known and accepted principle of explosion, which states all propositions can be deduced from contradictions, unless it also accepts trivialism, the notion that every proposition is true. However, because trivialism is instinctively false, the principle of explosion is almost always rejected by those who subscribe to dialetheism.

THOMAS HOBBES (1588–1679)

A new philosophical system

Thomas Hobbes was born on April 5, 1588, in Malmesbury, England. Though his father disappeared when he was young, Hobbes's uncle paid for his education, and by the time he was fourteen years old, Hobbes studied at Magdalen Hall in Oxford. In 1608, Hobbes left Oxford and became a tutor for the oldest son of Lord Cavendish of Hardwick. In 1631, while tutoring another family member of the Cavendish family, Hobbes began to focus on his philosophical ideas and wrote his first published piece, *Short Tract on First Principles*.

Hobbes's association with the Cavendish family proved to be quite beneficial. He was able to sit in on parliamentary debates; contribute to discussions about the king, landowners, and Parliament members; and get a firsthand look at how government was structured and influenced. During an incredibly tumultuous time between the monarchy and Parliament, Hobbes was a staunch monarchist and even wrote his first political philosophy, *The Elements of Law, Natural and Politic*, in defense of King Charles I. In the early 1640s, as the conflict escalated into what would become the English Civil Wars (1642–1651), Hobbes fled the country and moved to France, where he would remain for eleven years. It was while he lived in France that Hobbes produced his most important work (including his most famous book, *Leviathan*, published two years after the execution of King Charles I).

Thomas Hobbes was an incredibly individualistic thinker. During the English Civil Wars, while most in favor of the monarchy began to soften their arguments by expressing support for the Church of

England, Hobbes, who was the most prominent royalist, proclaimed his distaste for the church, which led him to become banned by the king's court. Even as a staunch supporter of the monarchy, Hobbes did not believe the king's right to rule was from God; rather, it was a social contract agreed upon by the people.

Hobbes was convinced that there needed to be an overhaul of philosophy, and set out to make a totalizing philosophical system that could provide an agreed-upon basis for absolutely all knowledge. The root of his philosophical system was his belief that all phenomena in the universe could be traced back to matter and motion. However, he rejected that the experimental method and observation of nature could act as a base for knowledge. Instead, his philosophy was deductive and based everything on universally accepted "first principles."

THE PHILOSOPHIES OF THOMAS HOBBES

Views on Knowledge

Hobbes believed that basing philosophy and science on the observations of nature alone was too subjective because humans have the ability to view the world in many different ways. He rejected the work of Francis Bacon and Robert Boyle, who used inductive reasoning from nature to draw scientific and philosophical conclusions. Instead, he believed the purpose of philosophy was to establish a system of truths that were based on foundational, universal principles that could be demonstrated by anyone through language and agreed upon by all.

In searching for a philosophy based on universal principles, Hobbes turned to geometry as a model and claimed it to be the first universal principle. Because of its deductive reasoning, Hobbes believed geometry to be a model of true science and used this notion of deductive reasoning to create his political philosophy.

Views on Human Nature

Thomas Hobbes did not believe in dualism or the existence of a soul. Humans, according to Hobbes, are like machines; made of material and whose functions could be explained by mechanical processes (for example, sensation is caused by the mechanical processes of the nervous system). As such, Hobbes claimed that humans avoid pain and pursue pleasure in an effort to seek out our own self-interest (which makes humans' judgment extremely unreliable), and that our thoughts and emotions are based on cause and effect and action-reaction. Hobbes believed that human judgment needs to be guided by science, which, in *Leviathan*, he refers to as "the knowledge of consequences."

Society, according to Hobbes, was a similar machine that, while artificial, also followed the same laws, and all phenomena in the entire universe could be explained through the interactions and motions of material bodies.

Fear, Hope, and the Social Contract

Hobbes did not believe morality exists in a human's natural state. So when he speaks of good and evil, he refers to "good" as anything people desire and "evil" as anything people avoid. Based on these definitions, Hobbes then goes on to explain various behaviors and emotions. Hope, according to Hobbes's definition, is the possibility of gaining some apparent good, and fear is recognizing that an apparent good cannot be attained (though this definition is only maintainable when considering humans outside of the constraints of laws and society). Since good and evil are based on individual desires, rules regarding what makes something good or evil cannot exist.

It is the constant back-and-forth between feelings of hope and fear that Hobbes believed was the defining principle of all human action, and he claimed that one of the two are present in all people at any given time.

Hobbes depicts the "state of nature" as humans having an instinctive desire to gain as much good and power as they possibly can. This desire and a lack of any laws that prevent one from harming others create a state of constant war. And this constant war in the state of nature means humans must be living in constant fear of one another. However, when reason and fear combine, it makes humans follow the state of nature (the desire to gain as much good as one can) and makes humans seek out peace. Furthermore, good and evil cannot exist until a society's supreme authority establishes these rules.

Hobbes claims the only way peace can truly be achieved is by coming together and creating a social contract in which a group of people agree to have one supreme authority rule over a commonwealth. Within the social contract, fear serves two purposes:

1. It creates the state of war within the state of nature so that a social contract is required.
2. It upholds the peace within a commonwealth (by allowing for the supreme authority to instill fear in everyone through punishing those who break the contract).

Plato was one of the foundational figures in Western philosophy. His musings took the form of dialogues—discussions that ranged across topics as diverse as art, ethics, metaphysics, and theatre. Plato is perhaps most well known for his Allegory of the Cave, although his work ranged far beyond this one thought experiment.

The symbol of yin and yang is a central one to the philosophy of Taoism. Tao, which means "way," is concerned primarily with understanding and yielding to the natural order and ebb and flow of existence.

Socrates was perhaps the first Western philosopher to focus on the value of human experience, instead of simply examining the world from a distance. He played a role in educating many of the brightest minds of his age, and his development of the Socratic method was one of the key milestones in all of human thought and knowledge.

David Hume was a leading proponent of empiricism, the idea that valid knowledge comes from experience. This basis in rational, empirical study set the stage for many of the scientific and philosophical advances of the later eighteenth century.

In philosophical terms, Buddhism examines the human failings that Buddhists believe lead to continual rebirth in the "false world" that we all inhabit. In order to escape the cycle of death and reincarnation, it is necessary to quench passion and desire, and to see the world clearly for what it is—the elusive enlightenment.

Gottfried Wilhelm Leibniz was one of the most influential and important seventeenth-century philosophers, a key voice in the development of rationalism. He was talented across a wide range of disciplines, however, and is credited with inventing calculus independent of Sir Isaac Newton, along with discovering the binary system.

I THINK, THEREFORE I AM

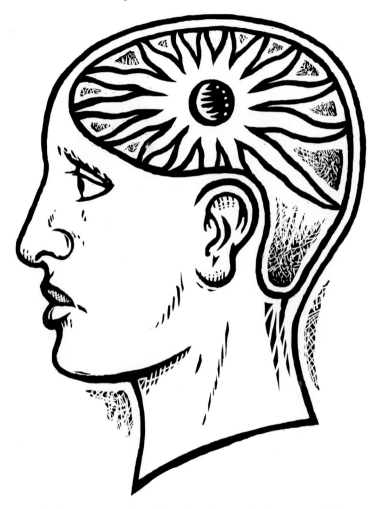

This image is an encapsulation of Descartes's famous "Cogito ergo sum" dictum—
"I think; therefore I am." This argument was the cornerstone of Descartes's philosophy,
and accepting this as fact allowed him to move outward and attempt to prove the existence
of God, a "philosophical perfection."

St. Thomas Aquinas wrote an incredible number of philosophical texts, which touched on many different subjects, ranging from natural philosophy and the work of Aristotle to theology and the Bible. His most famous and extensive work, *Summa Theologiae*, is where Aquinas's most famous philosophical text, the Five Ways, is found. In this, Aquinas sets out to prove the existence of God.

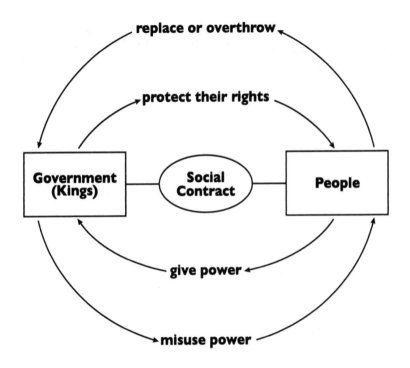

Views on Government

While, in his earlier works, Hobbes claimed society needs a supreme sovereign power, in *Leviathan*, Hobbes makes his stance clear: An absolute monarchy is the best type of government and the only type that can provide peace for all.

Hobbes believed that factionalism within society, such as rival governments, differing philosophies, or the struggle between church and state, only leads to civil war. Therefore, to maintain peace for all, everyone in a society must agree to have one authoritative figure that controls the government, makes the laws, and is in charge of the church.

PHILOSOPHY OF LANGUAGE

What is language?

Toward the end of the nineteenth century, as theories in logic began to advance and philosophies regarding the mind began to change drastically from previous accounts, a revolution in understanding language occurred. This event is referred to as the "linguistic turn." Philosophers began to focus on the meaning of language, the use of language, the cognition of language, and how language and reality relate to one another.

COMPOSITION OF A SENTENCE AND LEARNING

The philosophy of language attempts to understand how meaning comes about from the parts that make up a sentence. In order to understand the meaning of language, the relationship between entire sentences and parts that are meaningful need to first be examined. According to the principle of compositionality, a sentence can be understood based on an understanding of structure (syntax) and the meaning of the words.

There are two accepted methods in understanding how meaning comes about within a sentence:

Example of a Syntactic Tree

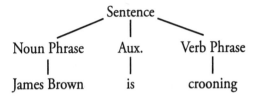

Example of (one kind of) Semantic Tree

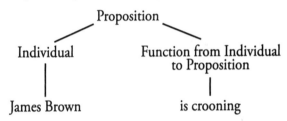

The syntactic tree focuses on grammar and words that make up the sentence, while the semantic tree focuses on meanings of words and the combinations of these meanings.

In regard to learning language, there are three main schools of thought:

1. **Innatism:** The notion that some syntactic settings are innate and based on certain parts of the mind.
2. **Behaviorism:** The notion that a very large amount of language is learned through conditioning.
3. **Hypothesis Testing:** The notion that children learn syntactic rules through postulation and testing hypotheses.

MEANING

The roots of the "linguistic turn" occurred in the mid-nineteenth century, as language started to be viewed as the focal point in representing the world and understanding belief, and philosophers began to place emphasis on the meaning of language.

John Stuart Mill

In his work in empiricism, John Stuart Mill examined the meaning of words in relation to the objects they refer to. Mill claimed that in order for words to hold meaning, one must be able to explain them based on experience. Therefore, words stand for impressions made from the senses.

While some disagreed with Mill's empiricist viewpoint, many philosophers agreed with Mill's belief that denotation should be the basis of meaning, rather than connotation.

Philosophical Definitions

DENOTATION: When the definition of a word is the literal meaning of what it is describing. For example, using the word *snake* to describe the actual reptile this word is affiliated with. **CONNOTATION:** When the definition of a word suggests a quality or attribute. For example, using the word *snake* to mean "evil."

John Locke

According to John Locke, words do not represent external things; rather, they represent ideas within the mind of the person saying them. While these ideas are presumed to then represent things,

Locke believed the accuracy of the representation does not affect that word's meaning.

With that in mind, Locke set out to eliminate the natural shortcomings of language that naturally arise. He suggested that people should never use words without having a clear idea of those words' meanings; people should attempt to identify the same meanings of words used by others so as to have a common vocabulary; people should be consistent with their use of words; and if a meaning of a word is unclear, one should then define it more clearly.

Gottlob Frege

The work of German philosopher and mathematician Gottlob Frege focused mainly on logic. However, as his investigations in logic became more in-depth, Frege realized that, to continue pursuing his work, he first needed to understand language. By doing so, he created some of the most groundbreaking work in the philosophy of language.

Frege questions identity, names, and the expression a = b. For example, Mark Twain is Samuel Clemens. However, if a = b is informative, how come a = a is trivial and doesn't actually provide any new information?

Frege believed that it is not simply the objects that are relevant to the meaning of a sentence, but how the objects are presented. Words refer to things in the external world—however, names hold more meaning than simply being references to objects. Frege broke sentences and expressions up into two parts: the sense and the reference (or meaning). To Frege, the sense of a sentence is the objective, universal, and abstract thought the sentence is expressing and the "mode of presentation" of the object that is being referred to. The reference, or meaning, of a sentence is the object in the real world that the sentence is referring to. The reference represents a truth-value (whether something is true or false) and is determined by senses.

Frege expresses this theory as a triangle:

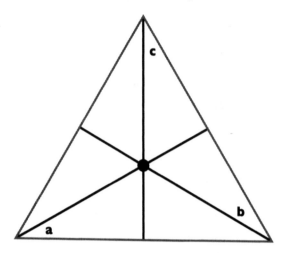

The intersection of line a and line b is the same as the intersection of line b and line c. Therefore, this statement is informative because we are presented with two different modes of presentation. To say the intersection of line a and line b is the same as the intersection of line a and line b only presents one single mode of presentation, and is therefore trivial.

Frege concludes that there are three parts to a name (though all three are not necessarily needed in every case):

1. **Sign:** The word or words used (for example, Mark Twain).
2. **Sense:** The way to get at what is being referred to by the sign (for example, the psychological implications we have of Mark Twain—he is a humorist; he is the author of *Tom Sawyer*; etc.).

3. **Referent:** The actual object being referred to (for example, Mark Twain is also Samuel Clemens, who is also the author of *Tom Sawyer*).

THE USE OF LANGUAGE

Intentionality is another important topic with regard to the philosophy of language. Intentionality is defined as the particular mental states that are directed toward objects or things in the real world. Intentionality is not about one's intention to do something or not do something, but rather, the ability of our thoughts to be *about* something. For example, you can have a belief *about* roller coasters, but a roller coaster itself cannot be *about* anything. Therefore, mental states like fear, hope, and desire have to be intentional because there must be an object that is being referenced.

Nineteenth-century German philosopher Franz Brentano argued that only mental phenomena could show intentionality. Later, twentieth-century philosopher John Searle questioned how the mind and language has the ability to force intentionality onto objects when such objects are not intentional on their own. In his theory of speech acts, Searle concludes that actions have intentionality as well, because language is a form of human behavior and an action on its own. Therefore, by saying something, one is actually performing an action, and intentionality is present in actions.

In a much-debated discussion on artificial intelligence, Searle argued that machines would never have the ability to think. Searle claimed that machines lack intentionality and that only an organized mind, like that of a human being, is able to perform intentionality.

METAPHYSICS

First philosophy

Aristotle was a firm believer in metaphysics. He referred to it as the "first philosophy," and in many regards, metaphysics is the foundation of all philosophies. Metaphysics focuses on the nature of being and existence, and asks very complicated and profound questions relating to God, our existence, if there is a world outside of the mind, and what reality is.

Originally, Aristotle broke metaphysics up into three branches, which continue to be the major branches of metaphysics to this day. They are:

1. **Ontology:** The study of existence and being, including mental and physical entities, and the study of change.
2. **Universal Science:** The study of logic and reasoning, considered to be the "first principles."
3. **Natural Theology:** The study of God, religion, spirituality, and creation.

EXISTENCE EXISTS

In metaphysics, existence is defined as a state of continued being. "Existence exists" is the famous axiom to come out of metaphysics; it simply states that there is something instead of nothing. The root of every thought a person ever has is the notion that he is aware of something, which is proof that something must exist. Therefore, if something must exist, that must mean that existence has to exist. Existence is necessary and required for there to be any type of knowledge.

When one denies the existence of something, he is saying that something does not exist. However, even the very act of denying can only be possible if existence exists. In order for anything to exist, it must have an identity. Everything that exists exists as something, for otherwise it would be nothing and would not exist.

In order for one to have a thought of being aware of something, one has to be conscious. Therefore, according to René Descartes, consciousness has to exist because one cannot deny the existence of his mind while using his mind to make that denial. However, Descartes's axiom was incorrect because he believed a person has the ability to be aware without there being something to be aware of. This cannot be the case, however.

Consciousness, rather, is the faculty to perceive what exists. Being conscious means one is perceiving something, so to function, consciousness requires that there be something outside of itself. Therefore, consciousness not only requires existence; it is also dependent upon existence. Descartes's axiom of consciousness as being aware of being conscious cannot, therefore, be the case because to be conscious requires the existence of something external.

OBJECTS AND PROPERTIES

In metaphysics, philosophers try to understand the nature of objects and the properties of these objects. According to metaphysics, the world is made up of things, known as objects or particulars, that can be either physical or abstract. These particulars share certain qualities or attributes in common with one another, and philosophers refer to these commonalities as universals or properties.

When philosophers attempt to explain whether properties can exist in more than one place simultaneously, they run across what is referred to as the "problem of universals." For example, a red apple and a red car can exist simultaneously, so is there some kind of property that exists that is "redness"? If redness does exist, what is it? Different schools of thought answer that question in their own ways:

- According to Platonic realism, redness does exist, but it exists outside of space and time.
- According to moderate forms of realism, redness exists within space and time.
- According to nominalism, universals like redness do not exist independently; they exist as names alone.

These ideas of existence and properties lead to one of the most important aspects of metaphysics: identity.

IDENTITY

In metaphysics, identity is defined as whatever makes an entity recognizable. All entities have specific characteristics and qualities that allow one to define and distinguish them from other entities. As Aristotle states in his law of identity, in order to exist, an entity must have a particular identity.

In discussing what the identity of an entity is, two very important concepts arise: change and causality.

Many identities can appear to be unstable. Houses can fall apart; eggs can break; plants can die; etc. However, these identities are not unstable; these objects are simply being affected by causality and are changing based on their identities. Therefore, identity needs to be explained based on the entity's building blocks and how those interact with one another. In other words, the identity of an entity is the sum of its parts. One can describe a house by describing how the different parts of wood, glass, and metal interact with one another in a specific way to form the house, or one can define a house's identity based on its formation of atoms.

To alter an identity, a change (caused by an action) needs to occur. The law of causality states that all causes have specific effects that are dependent on the original identities of the entities.

Currently, three main theories discuss the issue of change:

1. **Perdurantism:** This is the notion that objects are four-dimensional. According to perdurantism, objects have temporal parts (parts that exist in time), and at every moment of existence, objects only partly exist. So for example, there would be a series of stages for the life of a tree.
2. **Endurantism:** This is the notion that objects are the same and whole throughout every moment of the objects' history. So for example, as a tree loses leaves, it is still considered to be the same tree.
3. **Mereological Essentialism:** This notion explains that parts of an object are essential to that object. Therefore, the object is not able to persist if any of its parts change. According to mereological essentialism, when a tree loses its leaves, it is no longer the same tree. Because metaphysics touches on our existence and what it truly means to be in the world, it touches on a wide variety of philosophical issues. And it is for this very reason that metaphysics is often considered to be the foundation of philosophy, or "first philosophy."

JEAN-PAUL SARTRE (1905–1980)

Pioneer of existentialism

Jean-Paul Sartre was born on June 21, 1905, in Paris, France. When Sartre's father died in 1906, Sartre and his mother moved in with his mother's father, Karl Schweitzer, who was a respected philosophical and religious writer. His grandfather's religious beliefs proved to be a point of contention for Sartre growing up, and though he resented his grandfather's presence, he was open to being tutored by Schweitzer.

Sartre studied philosophy at the prestigious university École Normale Supérieure in 1924, and in 1928, he met fellow classmate and lifelong companion Simone de Beauvoir (who would go on to write *The Second Sex*, which is considered to be one of the most important feminist texts ever produced). Upon graduating, Sartre enlisted in the army and then took a teaching job in France. By 1933, Sartre had moved to Berlin to study philosophy with Edmund Husserl, and while in Berlin, he also became acquainted with Martin Heidegger. The work of these two men would have a profound impact on Sartre's own philosophy, and in 1938, Sartre's philosophical novel, *Nausea*, was published.

In 1939, at the beginning of World War II, Sartre was drafted into the French army. In 1940, Sartre was captured by the Germans and was held as a prisoner of war for nine months. During this time, Sartre began to write his most famous existential work, *Being and Nothingness*. Sartre returned to Paris in 1941, and two years later, *Being and Nothingness* was published, propelling Sartre's fame in the public eye and establishing him as a key intellectual of the post-war era.

Sartre then served as editor for the journal *Les Temps Modernes*, where he was able to continually write and hone his philosophy, focusing on the political and social world of the time and becoming a political activist. Sartre remained committed to political activism for the rest of his life. A staunch Socialist, Sartre supported the Soviet Union during the Cold War (even though he was critical of the totalitarianism that was featured in Sovietism), met with Fidel Castro and Che Guevara in support of Marxism, opposed the Vietnam War, and was famously an outspoken critic of France's colonization of Algeria.

Sartre was a prolific writer. In 1964, he was awarded the Nobel Prize in Literature, which he declined (making him the first person to ever do so), claiming that no writer should be turned into an institution and that the cultures of the East and West must be able to exchange with one another without the help of an institution. Throughout his extensive writing career, he wrote philosophical books, films, and plays.

THE PHILOSOPHICAL THEMES OF JEAN-PAUL SARTRE

While his pursuits in political activism took up his later life, his early work in existentialism is considered to be some of the most profound philosophical work ever produced.

Knowing the Self

Sartre believed every individual person to be a "being-for-itself" that has self-consciousness. According to Sartre, people do not have an essential nature. Rather, they have a self-consciousness and a consciousness, and these can always be changed. If a person believes that his place in society determines his sense of self or that his views cannot be changed, he is deceiving himself. Telling someone "that's just how I am" is also self-deception.

According to Sartre, self-actualization, the process of making something from what someone has already been made into, is always possible. To do so, one must recognize what Sartre calls the "facticity"—the realities (based on facts) that occur outside of the individual that are acting on him. One must also understand that he has a consciousness that exists independently from those realities.

Sartre believed the only type of truly authentic outlook is understanding that, while an individual is responsible for his consciousness, consciousness of self will never be identical to actual consciousness.

Being-in-Itself and Being-for-Itself

To Sartre, there are two types of being:

- *en-soi* (being-in-itself): Things that have an essence that is both definable and complete; however, they are not conscious of their complete essence or of themselves. For example, rocks, birds, and trees.
- *pour-soi* (being-for-itself): Things that are defined by the fact that they have consciousness and are conscious that they exist (like humans), and are also consciously aware that they do not have the complete essence associated with *en-soi*.

The Role of the Other

Sartre says that a person (or being-for-itself) only becomes aware of his own existence when he sees another being-for-itself observing him. Thus, people become consciously aware of their identity only when being viewed by others who also possess consciousness. Thus, a person only understands himself in relation to others.

Sartre goes on to claim that encountering the "Other" can be tricky at first because one might think that the other conscious being is objectifying him with regard to appearance, type, and essence (even if that is imagined). As a result, a person may then attempt to view Others as simple and definable objects that lack any individual consciousness. According to Sartre, it is from the idea of the Other that we see things like racism, sexism, and colonialism.

Responsibility

Sartre believed that all individuals have an essential freedom and that people are responsible for their actions, their consciousness, and all aspects of their self. Even if an individual wishes not to be held responsible for himself, according to Sartre, that is a conscious decision, and he is responsible for the results of his inaction.

Based on this notion, Sartre explains that ethics and morals are subjective and related to an individual's conscience. Therefore, there could never be any type of universal ethics or morality.

Freedom

As he began to focus more on politically inclined issues, Sartre examined how individual consciousness and freedom fit into social structures such as racism, sexism, colonialism, and capitalist exploitation. He said that those structures do not recognize individual consciousness and freedom, and instead, objectify people.

Sartre believed people always have freedom—no matter how objectified an individual is, the fact that freedom and consciousness exist means that individuals still have the ability to make something happen. To Sartre, the inherent freedom of consciousness is both a gift and a curse. While freedom can allow one to make a change and shape his life, there is also a responsibility that comes along with it.

FREE WILL

Can we act freely?

When discussing free will, philosophers look at two things:

1. What it means to choose freely
2. What the moral implications are of those decisions

However, upon examining these two notions further, more questions arise. Philosophers take many different approaches in trying to answer these questions.

COMPATIBILISM AND INCOMPATIBILISM

Those who believe in compatibilism (also known as soft determinism) believe that humans do have free will—however, this free will is viewed as being compatible with determinism (which is causal, and as a philosophy states that nothing is by chance; everything that happens is the result of what happened before, and everything about you and everything that you do is inevitable).

According to compatibilism, humans can be free agents (and have free will) when they are free of certain constraints. According to both determinism and compatibilism, peoples' personalities and characteristics are determined in ways that are out of their hands (genetics, upbringing, etc.). However, in compatibilism, the existence of these constraints does not mean one cannot also have free will, because compatibilism works off of those things that are determined.

The definition of free will in compatibilism is that one is free to choose how to act to whatever extent made possible by that person's makeup.

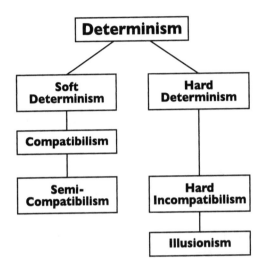

But then, if it is not determinism that is considered to be a constraint in compatibilism, what is the constraint? According to compatibilism, a constraint is any type of external coercion. Free will, therefore, is defined as freedom of action. As long as an individual is able to make his own decisions (even if those decisions are already determined) free of an external force (like imprisonment), then that person has free will.

Alternatively, some people do not believe in compatibilism. Those who believe incompatibilism to be true claim that determinism is simply incompatible with the notion of free will. For example, how can one have free will if every decision is predetermined from birth?

This does not necessarily mean that incompatibilism states free will does or does not exist. In fact, incompatibilism can be broken down into three types:

1. **Hard determinism** (which denies the existence of free will)
2. **Metaphysical libertarianism** (which states free will does exist and denies the existence of compatibilism)
3. **Pessimistic incompatibilism** (which states that neither free will nor compatibilism is true)

The previous image shows several offshoots of compatibilism and incompatibilism:

- **Semicompatibilism** is the notion that determinism is compatible with moral responsibility.
- **Hard incompatibilism** is the belief that moral responsibility and free will are not compatible with determinism.
- **Illusionism** is the belief that free will is just an illusion.

Incompatibilists who deny determinism accept that random events must therefore occur in the world (be they mental, biological, physical, etc.), and thus, randomness and accidents do exist. This then creates chains of unpredictable futures (as opposed to the one predestined future in determinism).

Another form of incompatibilism, metaphysical libertarianism, comes in four different branches of causality:

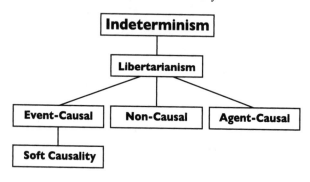

- **Event-causal libertarianism** is the notion that some events are not as predictable from earlier events and are uncaused.
- **Soft causality** is the belief that most events are determined, while some events are not as predictable.
- **Agent-causal libertarianism** is the belief that new causal chains can begin that are not determined by past events or laws of nature.
- **Non-causal libertarianism** is the idea that in order to make decisions, no cause is needed at all. Those who believe in compatibilism believe humans can be free agents (and have free will) when they are free of certain constraints, and that personalities and characteristics are determined in ways that are out of their hands (such as genetics or upbringing), while incompatibilists deny that determinism plays a role in free will and accept that random events and accidents must therefore occur in the world (be they mental, biological, physical, etc.).

RESPONSIBILITY

When discussing free will, one must also discuss the idea of responsibility; particularly the distinction between responsibility and moral responsibility. Responsibility is when one takes on a task or burden and accepts the associated consequences. For example, if you take on the responsibility of organizing a conference for work, then you not only take on the task of organizing the event, but you are also taking on the responsibility of its outcome; be it a success or failure. This is responsibility. Moral responsibility, on the other hand, is responsibility based on one's moral codes. Let's say that on the day of the conference, a big snowstorm hits and none of the speakers can make the conference. You are responsible for the success or failure of the conference, but are you morally responsible for the conference's failure?

It seems that humans do in fact *feel* responsible for their actions. But why is this the case? If one's actions are determined by events, that is to say, one's actions are the result of events and have been planned since before birth, then libertarians would ask why people feel responsible for their actions. Similarly, if one's actions are totally random and determined entirely by chance, determinists would wonder why people feel responsible for their actions. Together, these questions create the standard argument against free will.

Yet humans *do* feel responsible for their actions. So if a person is responsible for his actions, this must mean that responsibility is caused by something that is within all of us. Therefore, *a prerequisite of responsibility is free will*, and not the other way around. And furthermore, *a prerequisite of moral responsibility is responsibility*, and not the other way around. One does not need moral responsibility to have responsibility, but one certainly needs responsibility to have moral responsibility.

THE REQUIREMENTS OF FREE WILL

Requirements of free will should ideally satisfy both libertarianism (allowing for the unpredictability needed for freedom to occur) and determinism (allowing for the causality needed for moral responsibility to occur). It is here we see how *free* meets *will*.

The Randomness Requirement

The randomness, or freedom, requirement states that indeterminism is true and chance exists. Actions are considered to be unpredictable and are not caused by external events; rather, they come from us. In order for there to be free will, there must also be alternative possibilities, and after an action has been performed, the notion that it could have been done a different way must be present. Therefore, according to the randomness requirement, people create new causal chains and new information is produced.

The Determinism Requirement

The determinism, or will, requirement states that adequate determinism (determinism that has the ability to allow for statistical predictability) must be true and that our actions cannot be directly caused by chance. Furthermore, a person's will must also be adequately determined, and one's actions have to be causally determined by an individual's will.

The Moral Responsibility Requirement

The moral responsibility requirement is the result of combining the randomness requirement with the determinism requirement. It states that people are morally responsible for their actions because there are alternative possibilities. One could have done things in a different way—actions come from us, and our actions are causally determined by one's will. The issue of free will is one that affects all of us. Are we truly free when we make a decision? What are the implications that come about from our decisions?

PHILOSOPHY OF HUMOR

The serious side of laughter

When philosophers look at humor, they attempt to explain its function, how it hinders or enhances human relations, and what makes something humorous. Traditionally, many philosophers have looked down upon humor, and Plato even referred to laughter as an emotion that interrupted one's rational self-control. Plato called laughter malicious, and described enjoying comedy as being a type of scorn. In Plato's ideal state, humor would be under tight control; the Guardian class would have to avoid laughing; and no "composer of comedy" would be allowed to make citizens laugh.

Plato's objections to humor and laughter carried over to Christian thinkers and, later, to European philosophers. In the Bible, laughter is often referred to as a source of hostility, and in monasteries, laughter was condemned. As thought reformed in the Middle Ages, the view of humor remained the same. Puritans despised humor and laughter, and when they came to rule England in the seventeenth century, comedies were completely outlawed.

THEORIES ON HUMOR

These ideas of comedy and laughter are also found in the work of Western philosophy. In Thomas Hobbes's *Leviathan*, Hobbes calls humans competitive and individualistic, and says that by laughing, we are expressing superiority through grimaces. Similarly, in Descartes's *Passions of the Soul*, laughter is considered to be an expression of ridicule and scorn. Here are some schools of thought about humor.

The Superiority Theory

From the work of Hobbes and Descartes comes the superiority theory. According to this theory, when one laughs, he is expressing feelings of superiority. These feelings can be expressed over others or even over one's former state.

This philosophical theory was the dominant one until the eighteenth century, when philosopher Francis Hutcheson critiqued the ideas of Thomas Hobbes. Hutcheson claimed that feeling superior is neither a sufficient nor a necessary explanation of laughter and that there are cases when one laughs in which feelings of glory or self-comparison are simply not present. For example, one can laugh at a figure of speech that seems odd.

In other cases of humor, we see the points Hutcheson was making. When we watch Charlie Chaplin, we laugh at the incredibly clever stunts he performed. Laughing at these stunts does not require one to compare himself to Chaplin, and even if one does compare himself, he does not laugh because he believes himself to be superior.

People also have the ability to laugh at themselves without laughing at their former selves, which the superiority theory cannot explain. If one searches for his glasses only to discover that he has been wearing them the whole time, this is reason to laugh. However, this type of laughter does not fit with the model set forth by the superiority theory.

The Relief Theory

One theory that came about during the eighteenth century that weakens the superiority theory is known as the relief theory. The relief theory claims laughter behaves in the nervous system the way a pressure-relief valve works in a steam boiler.

The relief theory first appears in 1709 in Lord Shaftesbury's *An Essay on the Freedom and Wit of Humor*, and it is notable for being the very first time humor is discussed as being a sense of funniness.

During this time period, scientists understood that the brain has nerves that connect it to muscles and sense organs. However, scientists also believed nerves carried liquids and gases, like blood and air, which they referred to as "animal spirits." In *An Essay on the Freedom and Wit of Humor*, Shaftesbury claims these animal spirits build pressure within the nerves, and that laughter is responsible for releasing the animal spirits.

As science advanced and the biology of the nervous system became clearer, the relief theory adapted. According to philosopher Herbert Spencer, emotions actually take on a physical form within the body, and this is known as nervous energy. Spencer claimed that nervous energy leads to muscular motion. For example, the nervous energy from anger creates small movements (like clenching your fist), and as the anger increases, so too do the muscle movements (like throwing a punch). Thus, the nervous energy builds up and is then released.

According to Spencer, laughter also releases nervous energy. However, Spencer identifies one major difference between the release of nervous energy from laughter versus other emotions: The muscle movements caused by laughter are not the beginning stages of larger actions. Laughter, unlike emotions, does not revolve around having a motivation to do something. The bodily movements associated with laughter are simply a release of pent-up nervous energy.

Spencer then goes on to claim that the nervous energy that laughter releases is the energy of inappropriate emotions. For example, if you are reading a story that starts off by causing anger but then ends in a joke, the anger from the beginning needs to be re-evaluated. So that nervous energy, which is no longer applicable, is then released in the form of laughter.

Perhaps the most famous version of the relief theory is Sigmund Freud's. He looked at three different types of situations that would result in laughter being the release of nervous energy from a psychological activity: "joking," "the comic," and "humor." According to Freud, in joking (the telling of jokes and funny banter), the unnecessary energy represses feelings; in the comic (for example, laughing at a clown), the unnecessary energy is that energy devoted to thinking (a large amount of energy is required to understand the clumsy movements of the clown, while a small amount of energy is required for us to perform our own movements smoothly, thus creating a surplus of energy); and in humor, the release of energy is similar to the release described by Herbert Spencer (an emotion becomes prepared, then is never utilized and needs to be laughed off).

The Incongruity Theory

The second challenge to the superiority theory, which also came about during the eighteenth century, is the incongruity theory. According to this theory, laughter is caused by the perception of something that is incongruous, meaning it violates our expectations and our mental patterns. This is currently the dominant theory explaining humor; it has been backed by influential philosophers and psychologists, including Søren Kierkegaard, Immanuel Kant, and Arthur Schopenhauer (it was even hinted at by Aristotle).

James Beattie, the first philosopher to use the term *incongruous* when referencing the philosophy of humor, claimed that laughter is caused by the mind taking notice of two or more incongruous circumstances that unite in one complex assemblage. Kant, who never used the term *incongruous*, examined how jokes toy with one's expectations. To Kant, jokes (for example, a setup followed by a punch line) evoke, shift, and then dissipate one's thoughts. Kant notes that the thrust of ideas then creates a physical thrust of one's internal organs, and this is, in turn, an enjoyable physical stimulation.

Following Kant's work, Arthur Schopenhauer's version of the incongruity theory claimed that the sources of humor are the abstract rational knowledge we have of something and the sense perceptions of those things. Schopenhauer claimed humor is the result of suddenly realizing the incongruity between a concept of something and the perception of something that should be the same.

As the theory of incongruity developed throughout the twentieth century, a flaw of older versions was discovered—the implication that, with regard to humor, the perception of incongruity is sufficient. This cannot be, because instead of amusement, one could theoretically experience anger, disgust, or fear, for example. Therefore, humorous amusement is not simply responding to incongruity; it is enjoying it.

Nervous Energy?

While there is a connection between laughter and muscles, almost no philosopher today explains humor as a release of pent-up nervous energy.

One of the most recent forms of incongruity, created by Michael Clark, states that first one perceives something to be incongruous; then one enjoys perceiving it; and then one enjoys the incongruity. The incongruity is enjoyed simply for itself (or at least some of it). This theory does a better job of explaining humor than the relief and the superiority theories, since it accounts for all types of humor.

THE ENLIGHTENMENT

Defying tradition

The Enlightenment refers to a radical shift in thought that occurred in Europe (particularly France, Germany, and Britain) during the late seventeenth and eighteenth centuries. This movement completely revolutionized the ways in which people viewed philosophy, science, politics, and society as a whole, and forever changed the shape of Western philosophy. Philosophers began to defy tradition and the pre-established thoughts of the ancient Greeks, which opened the floodgates to a new form of philosophical inquiry—one based on human knowledge and reason.

ORIGINS OF THE ENLIGHTENMENT: THE SCIENTIFIC REVOLUTION

The beginning of the Enlightenment can be traced to the 1500s, when the scientific revolution started in Europe. From 500 to 1350, very little had changed with regard to science. Belief systems and teachings were based on the work of the ancient Greeks, and these philosophies had been incorporated into the doctrine of the Catholic Church. When the Renaissance occurred, there was suddenly a renewed interest in the natural world. As people discovered their findings did not match the doctrine of the church (which had, up until that point, been accepted as true), more people began to investigate the world around them, and scientific discoveries relating to the natural world flourished.

This scientific exploration reached its apex during the 1500s and 1600s, in what is known as the scientific revolution. Advancements in science and mathematics from Nicolaus Copernicus, Johannes Kepler, Sir Isaac Newton, and Galileo Galilei not only questioned the work of Aristotle and the church; they made people view nature and humanity in completely different ways. The introduction of the scientific method, which is based on observation and experimentation, allowed scientists to explain various theories through the use of reason and logic, and removed tradition from science.

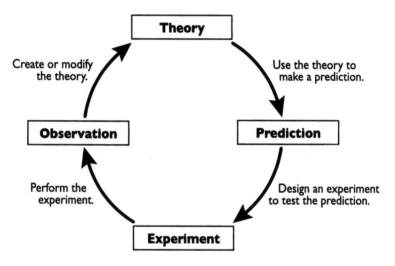

STUDY OF TRUTH

Philosophers during the Enlightenment set out to discover truths about nature, knowledge, and humanity. They did this through several different channels.

Skepticism

During the Enlightenment, skepticism played a key role in many philosophical advancements due to the fact that the very nature of the movement was to question established truths. Philosophers used skepticism as a tool to advance new sciences. When Descartes tried to create a new system of knowledge in his *Meditations on First Philosophy*, he made a secure foundation by using skepticism to determine which principles could be known as true with absolute certainty. Since the Enlightenment had roots in being critical and suspicious of doctrines, it only made sense for skepticism to influence the philosophies of the thinkers of this time.

Empiricism

The Enlightenment is sometimes referred to as the "Age of Reason," and empiricism, the belief that all of our knowledge comes from our experiences, played a key role in the history of the movement. While philosophers of this time did not see reason as its own source of knowledge, they explored human cognitive faculties (the abilities of the human mind) in new ways. Perhaps the most influential empiricist to come out of this time period was John Locke, whose most important theory was that the mind is a *tabula rasa*, or blank slate, at birth and that only when one has experiences does one begin to form knowledge.

The other major empiricist to come out of the Enlightenment was Sir Isaac Newton, who would go on to completely revolutionize science and mathematics (including creating calculus and identifying the existence of gravity). Newton's research began with observations of phenomena in nature, and he then used induction to find the mathematical principles that would be able to describe such phenomena. As the difference between Newton's "bottom-up" approach (which started with an observation from a phenomena in nature and then used the process of induction to create a mathematic law or principle, and led to successful results) and the approach of identifying first principles (which was often unending and never seemed to achieve desirable results) became clear, many philosophers during the Enlightenment began to favor the Newtonian method in their efforts to acquire knowledge.

Rationalism

One of the most significant philosophical changes that came about during the Enlightenment was the embracing of rationalism (the notion that we gain knowledge independent of the senses). The work of René Descartes, who attempted to find fundamental truths by assuming propositions to be false and by casting doubt on the senses, was particularly influential. Not only did Descartes question the ideas of Aristotle; he radically changed how one could view knowledge, which made way for new forms of science.

Through Cartesian philosophy (the term for René Descartes's views), various controversial questions arose from the intellectual community:

- Are the body and mind two substances that are separate and distinct from one another?
- How are the two related (with regard to both the human body and the unified world)?
- What role does God play in cementing our knowledge?

It is from the various questions posed by Cartesian philosophy that Baruch Spinoza, one of the Enlightenment's most influential philosophers, emerged.

Baruch Spinoza tackled the Cartesian theory of dualism and developed the theory of ontological monism (the notion that there is only one kind of substance, be it God or nature, that has two attributes that correspond to the mind and body). By identifying God with nature and denying the existence of a supreme being, Baruch Spinoza lays the foundation of the naturalism and atheism that can be seen throughout the philosophies of the Enlightenment.

In addition to Descartes and Spinoza, there were several other key philosophers of the Enlightenment that focused on rationalism. In Germany, one of the most influential philosophers was Gottfried Wilhelm Leibniz, who emphasized the principle of sufficient reason—the idea that there must be a sufficient reason for the existence of everything that exists. The principle of sufficient reason plays into the very ideals of the Enlightenment, as it presents the universe as being completely intelligible through the use of reason.

Based on Leibniz's work, Christian Wolff set out to answer the question of how the principle of sufficient reason could be grounded through the use of logic and the use of the principle of noncontradiction (which posits that a statement can never be true and false at the exact same time). Wolff did so by creating a rationalist system of knowledge, with the goal of showing that first principles, known as *a priori*, could demonstrate the truths of science. What makes the work of Wolff quintessential to the Enlightenment movement is not that he attempted to use reason to prove his argument; it's that he attempted to prove his argument using human reason.

AESTHETICS

During the Enlightenment, modern philosophical aesthetics first appears and flourishes. German philosopher Alexander Baumgarten, who had been a student of Christian Wolff, created and named aesthetics. According to Baumgarten, aesthetics was a science of the beautiful. Baumgarten equates his science of the beautiful with a science of the sensible—therefore, aesthetics was created as a science of sensible cognition. The Enlightenment embraced aesthetics for several reasons: the movement revolved around a rediscovery of the senses and the value of pleasure, and as art and art criticism flourished, the notion of beauty became extremely important among philosophers. The way in which we come to understand beauty, it was believed, reveals information about the rational order of nature.

German Rationalism

In Germany during the eighteenth century, aesthetics was largely based on Christian Wolff's rationalist metaphysics. Wolff was a proponent of the classic principle that beauty is truth. To Wolff, beauty is truth interpreted as feeling pleasure. Wolff sees beauty as that which has perfection. This perfection then leads to harmony and order. When one deems something beautiful (through feelings of pleasure), one is sensing some sort of perfection or harmony. Thus, the sensitive cognition of perfection is beauty. Wolff states that while beauty may relate to the objective features of those things around us, opinions on beauty are relative based on one's sensibility.

French Classicism

The French outlook on beauty during the Enlightenment was very much inspired by Descartes's model of the physical universe (deducing knowledge from prior knowledge in order to establish a single principle). Like German rationalism, French classicism based aesthetics on the classic principle that beauty is truth. Truth, for French philosophers, was viewed as objective rational order.

Philosophers viewed art as an imitation of nature in its ideal state, and in French classicism, aesthetics was modeled from the science of nature. Like Descartes's model, philosophers of French classicism attempted to systematize aesthetics in search of a universal principle.

Subjectivism and Empiricism

While the basis of aesthetics was formed in France and Germany, some of the most important work regarding aesthetics during the Enlightenment occurred in England and Scotland. Through empiricism and subjectivism, the understanding of aesthetics shifted to the viewer's understanding of beauty, in which both the experience of and the response to beauty were examined.

One of the major figures of this time, Lord Shaftesbury, agreed with the classic principle that beauty is truth. However, Shaftesbury did not believe this truth to be an objective rational order that one has the ability of knowing. To Shaftesbury, the response to aesthetics is that of a disinterested unegoistic pleasure, meaning it is independent of one's thoughts on how to promote his own self-interest (this revelation would pave the way for his theory on ethics based on the same idea). He claimed that beauty is a type of harmony that is free from the human mind, and that our immediate understanding of beauty is a form of participation with this harmony.

Shaftesbury then shifted his focus to the nature of one's response to beauty, and believed that this response elevated one morally, above self-interest. By shifting away from what makes something beautiful and toward the behavior of human nature with regard to beauty, Shaftesbury connected aesthetics with beauty, morality, and ethics and furthered the interest in human nature that had become associated with the Enlightenment.

As the Enlightenment progressed, later philosophers such as Immanuel Kant and David Hume contributed immensely to notions of empiricism and subjectivity, specifically with regard to the role of imagination.

POLITICS, ETHICS, AND RELIGION

The Enlightenment is perhaps most significant for its accomplishments in politics. During this time, three distinct revolutions occurred: the English Revolution, the American Revolution, and the French Revolution. As philosophers during the Enlightenment began to shift toward thoughts regarding human nature and became critical of established truths from the church and monarchy, the sociopolitical atmosphere also fell under scrutiny.

Sympathizers of these revolutions believed that the political and social authority was based on obscure traditions and religious myths, and they began to spread ideas of freedom, equality, human rights, and the need for a legitimate political system. Philosophers came to not only criticize government; they also created theories on what government *should* be like. It is here that we see people start to embrace ideas such as the right to religious freedom and the need for a political system with checks and balances. During this time, the political works of John Locke and Thomas Hobbes were the most influential.

As outlooks on politics and society began to change, so too did the way people viewed ethics and religion. With the increase of industrialization and urbanization, as well as the bloody wars fought in the name of religion, people (and certainly philosophers) began to question the motivations behind happiness, morality, and religion.

Instead of finding happiness by uniting with God or determining what makes something good based on what one's religion tells him, philosophers began to turn toward human nature and asked questions like: What would make one happy in this life?

Philosophers of the Enlightenment called for religion to rid itself of superstition, supernaturalism, and fanaticism and advocated for a more rational form. Anger toward the Catholic Church grew, and Protestantism began to grow in popularity. Religion during the Enlightenment began to take on four types:

1. **Atheism:** The idea, as stated by Denis Diderot, that humans should look not toward a supernatural being to discover the principles of natural order, but rather, within their own natural processes. Atheism was more common in France than in any other location during the Enlightenment.

2. **Deism:** This is the belief that there is a supreme being that created and governs the universe and has always had a plan for creation since its inception; however, this supreme being will not interfere with creation. Deism is most commonly thought of as the religion associated with the Enlightenment. Deism rejects the idea of miracles or special revelations, and instead argues that natural light is the true proof that there is a supreme being. Deists rejected the divinity of Jesus Christ, instead claiming him to be more like an excellent moral teacher. Deism also allowed for new discoveries in natural science, believing that God created this order.

3. **Religion of the Heart:** This is the belief that the God associated with deism is too rationalistic and distant from the constant struggles of humanity (and therefore, not serving the purpose religion is supposed to serve). Religion of the heart, notably embraced by

philosophers Rousseau and Shaftesbury, is a religion based on human sentiments. While sometimes considered to be a form of deism, religion of the heart is a "natural" religion, notable for its lack of "artificial forms of worship" and metaphysical grounding. Instead, emphasis is placed on natural human emotions.

4. **Fideism:** One of the single most important works to come out of the Enlightenment was David Hume's *Dialogues Concerning Natural Religion*. In *Dialogues*, which was published in 1779 after Hume's death, Hume (an atheist) criticizes the supposition that the world must have been created and authored by a supreme being because human existence and reason exist. Fideism states that no matter what, rational criticism cannot get rid of religious belief because religious belief is so "natural." Essentially, according to fideism, one does not need reasons to have religious belief; all one needs is faith. Some forms of fideism even go so far as to say that religious beliefs can be legitimate even if those beliefs oppose or conflict with reason. Through its rejection of the traditional, pre-established thought of the ancient Greeks and its emphasis on human knowledge and reason, the Enlightenment completely revolutionized the ways in which people viewed philosophy, science, politics, and society as a whole, and forever changed the shape of Western philosophy.

FRIEDRICH NIETZSCHE (1844–1900)

Life-affirmation

Friedrich Nietzsche was born on October 15, 1844, in Röcken, Germany. Nietzsche's father, a Lutheran pastor, died when Nietzsche was just four years old. Six months after his father's passing, Nietzsche's two-year-old brother died, leaving Nietzsche with his mother and two sisters. Nietzsche later said that the passing of his father and brother had a profound impact on him.

From the age of fourteen to nineteen, Friedrich Nietzsche attended one of the best boarding schools in Germany, and as he continued his education at the University of Bonn and the University of Leipzig, he gravitated toward philology (an academic discipline that revolved around the interpretations of biblical and classical texts). During this time, Nietzsche, who had been composing music since he was a teenager, became acquainted with famous composer Richard Wagner (who also happened to be an idol of Nietzsche's), and the close friendship that resulted between the two men would prove to have an incredible impact on Nietzsche throughout his life (twenty years later, Nietzsche would recall their friendship as being the "greatest achievement" of his life). By the time he was twenty-four years old, having not even completed his doctorate, Nietzsche was offered a faculty position at the University of Basel department of philology.

After a brief stint serving as a medical orderly in 1870 during the Franco-Prussian War (where he contracted dysentery, syphilis, and diphtheria), Nietzsche returned to the University of Basel, and in 1872, Nietzsche published his first book, *The Birth of Tragedy*. The book, while praised by Wagner, was met with negative criticism, particularly by Ulrich von Wilamowitz-Möllendorff, who would go on to become one of the leading German philologists of the time.

Nietzsche remained at the University of Basel until 1879. By 1878, it had become clear that Nietzsche was more interested in philosophy than philology, and his book *Human, All-Too-Human* marks the shift in his philosophical style (and the end of his friendship with Wagner, whose anti-Semitism and German nationalism disgusted Nietzsche). At the age of thirty-four, Nietzsche's health had deteriorated so much that he had to resign from the university.

From 1878 to 1889, as his health severely declined, Nietzsche moved around between German, Swiss, and Italian cities and wrote eleven books. On January 3, 1889, Nietzsche suffered from a nervous breakdown (possibly as a result of syphilis) when he watched a man whip a horse on the street. Nietzsche collapsed on the street and never regained his sanity. He would spend the next eleven years in a vegetative state until his death on August 25, 1900.

THE PHILOSOPHICAL THEMES OF FRIEDRICH NIETZSCHE

During his period of insanity, Nietzsche's half-sister, Elisabeth Förster-Nietzsche, cared for him. Elisabeth, who had been married to a prominent German anti-Semite and nationalist, selectively published Nietzsche's writings. Though completely unaware, Nietzsche had taken on celebrity status in Germany and was viewed later as a Nazi icon because what was published was a misleading selection of his work that was then used to promote the Nazi ideology. It was only once World War II ended that the world came to know the true beliefs of Friedrich Nietzsche.

Nihilism

Nietzsche is perhaps most famous for his quote, "God is dead." During the late nineteenth century, with the rise of the German state and advancements in science, many German philosophers viewed their present-day life with great optimism. Nietzsche, on the other hand, viewed these as troubling times marked by a fundamental crisis in values.

In his book, *Thus Spoke Zarathustra*, Nietzsche tells the story of a man named Zarathustra who, at the age of thirty, goes into the wilderness and enjoys it so much, he decides to live there for the next ten years. Upon returning to society, he declares God to be dead. From *Thus Spoke Zarathustra*, Nietzsche argued that the advancements of science made it so that people no longer turned to the prominent sets of values brought about by Christianity, and that there was no longer that powerful grasp on civilization, brought about by Christianity, that determines what makes something good and what makes something evil.

While he was actually a critic of Christianity, Nietzsche was an even larger critic of atheism, and feared it would be the next logical step. Nietzsche did not claim that science introduces a new set of values to people that replaces those values set forth by Christianity. Instead, he claimed that it is nihilism, the abandonment of any and all beliefs, that will come to replace the moral code set forth by Christianity.

Nietzsche believed that there is always a need for people to identify a source of value and meaning, and he concluded that if science was not that source, it would appear in other ways, such as aggressive nationalism. Nietzsche did not argue that there is a need to return to the traditions of Christianity. Rather, Nietzsche wanted to discover how to get out of this form of nihilism through an affirmation of life.

The Will to Power

Nietzsche's theory of the will to power can be broken up into two parts.

First, Nietzsche believed that everything in this world is in flux, and that a fixed being simply does not exist. Matter, knowledge, truth, and so on, is always changing, and the very core of this change is something known as the "will to power." The universe, according to Nietzsche, is made up of wills.

Second, the will to power is an individual's fundamental drive for power, which comes about through dominance and independence. The will to power is much stronger than the will to sex or the will to survive, and it can appear in different ways. While the will to power, according to Nietzsche, could appear as violence or physical dominance, it could also be turned inward and make one pursue mastery of his own self (as opposed to mastery of someone else).

Nietzsche believed that the notion of the ego or soul is simply a grammatical fiction. To Nietzsche, "I" is actually a mix of competing wills that constantly and chaotically try to overcome each other. Since the world is in flux and change is the most fundamental part of life, any attempts at viewing life as objective and fixed, whether in regard to philosophy, science, or religion, are viewed as life-denying.

Therefore, in order to live based on a life-affirming philosophy, one must embrace change and understand that change is the only constant.

The Role of Man

According to Nietzsche, there are animals, humans, and then the overman. When humans learned to control their instincts and natural impulses in order to attain greater gains (like civilizations, knowledge, and spirituality), they stopped being animals. Our will to power shifted from outward (controlling others) to inward (self-mastery); however, this process of self-mastery is difficult, and there is a constant temptation for humanity to give up (two such examples of humanity giving up, according to Nietzsche, are nihilism and Christian morality). In attempting to gain self-mastery, humans are on their way to becoming the overman, an entity that possesses self-mastery (which is lacking in animals) and good conscience (which is lacking in humans). The overman has a deep love of life and willingly accepts the constant struggle and suffering without ever complaining. Therefore, according to Nietzsche, humanity is not the destination; it is a transition into becoming the overman.

Truth

Nietzsche believed that "truth," the idea that there can only be one correct way to consider something, is proof that our thought process has become inflexible. According to Nietzsche, being flexible and recognizing that there can be more than one way to consider a matter is a sign of a healthy mind, and to have an inflexible mind is to say "no" to life.

Values

In *Beyond Good and Evil*, Nietzsche attempts to expose morality's psychological foundations. To Nietzsche, humans would be a healthier species if they did not have morality. He equated morality to fiction, and believed that values needed to be re-evaluated, for they are not objective. Nietzsche was particularly critical of Christian morality, and claimed that on a fundamental level, Christian morality is opposed to life and even an enemy of life. For example, according to Nietzsche, Christianity's notion of the afterlife devalues an individual's natural instincts and makes this life not seem as important, therefore promoting weakness.

In exposing the truth of morality, Nietzsche did not wish to replace Christian morality with some other form. Rather, he believed that, after realizing the truth behind morality, people would start to become more honest and realistic with regard to their motives and attitude toward life.

Eternal Recurrence

Perhaps Nietzsche's most intricate theory was his metaphysical theory of eternal recurrence. While complex, the core of his theory, like the rest of his work, revolves around an affirmation of life.

The idea of eternal recurrence has been around for centuries. A classic depiction of eternal recurrence from the Renaissance era is the Ouroboros, a dragon or snake eating its own tail.

One part of Nietzsche's theory of eternal recurrence is the notion that time is cyclical, meaning people will live each moment of their entire life over and over an endless amount of times, and each time will be the same. Every moment one experiences, therefore, occurs for an eternity, and we should embrace this fact and feel supreme joy about this.

The second part of Nietzsche's theory of eternal recurrence is that "being" does not exist because everything is constantly changing—therefore, everything is constantly "becoming." Nietzsche asserts that reality is intertwined and that we cannot distinguish "things" from other "things" due to the fact that everything is constantly changing. Therefore, one cannot judge one part of reality without judging all of reality. By coming to terms with the fact that our lives are in a constant state of becoming, we can either say "yes" or "no" to all of life. Considered to be one of the first existentialist philosophers, Friedrich Nietzsche had an influence on philosophy that was truly incredible. Above all else, Nietzsche's emphasis of "life-affirmation" and his challenges to morality and Christianity made him one of the most important philosophers of his time.

THE SORITES PARADOX

Little-by-little

The sorites paradox is another famous paradox created by Eubulides of Miletus. This paradox tackles the idea of vagueness. The word *sorites* comes from the Greek word *soros*, which means "heap." The sorites paradox states:

Imagine you have a heap of sand. While a single grain of sand does not make a heap, many grains, like 1,000,000 grains, for example, do make a heap.

1. If you were to remove a single grain of sand from the 1,000,000 grains of sand, then you would still have a heap.
2. If you were to remove another grain of sand, then you would still have a heap.
3. If you were to remove another grain of sand, then you would still have a heap.

Eventually, you can remove enough grains of sand so that it is no longer considered a heap, but at what point is that the case? Is 500 grains of sand still considered a heap but 499 grains of sand not?

The sorites paradox is also seen in another paradox created by Eubulides: the Bald Man. This paradox states:

1. If a man has one hair on his head, then he is considered bald.
2. If a man that has one hair on his head is considered bald, then a man with two hairs on his head is considered bald.

3. If a man that has two hairs on his head is considered bald, then a man with three hairs on his head is considered bald.

Therefore, a man with 1,000,000 hairs on his head is considered bald.

Even though a man with 1,000,000 hairs would certainly not be considered bald, according to logic, he should be considered as such. So at what point is the man no longer considered bald?

Philosophers Gottlob Frege and Bertrand Russell argued that ideal language should have precision and that natural language has a defect, vagueness. By getting rid of vagueness, one would eliminate soritical terms, thus getting rid of the sorites paradox.

Later, American philosopher Willard van Orman Quine believed vagueness could be eliminated from natural language entirely. While this would affect ordinary ways in which people talk, the "sweet simplicity," as Quine describes it, would be worth it.

PROPOSED SOLUTIONS

There are four responses that philosophers typically use to explain the sorites paradox:

1. Denying that logic is applicable to the sorites paradox
2. Denying some of the premises within the sorites paradox
3. Denying the validity of the sorites paradox
4. Accepting the sorites paradox as sound

Let's look at each possible solution.

Denying That Logic Is Applicable to the Sorites Paradox

Denying that logic is applicable to the sorites paradox does not seem to be the best possible solution. It seems that in order for logic to have any impact, it must be applied to natural language and not only to an ideal form of language. Therefore, the soritical terms cannot be avoided and must be dealt with in another way.

Denying Some Premises

Denying some of the premises of the sorites paradox is the most common solution today. In these solutions, logic can be applied to natural language; however, there are issues regarding the premises on which the sorites paradox is based.

The Epistemic Theory

In the epistemic theory, one conditional is assumed to be false and there is a certain cutoff point in any sorites paradox where the predicate no longer applies (and instead, the negation applies). If we were to again use the Bald Man paradox as an example:

1. A man that has one hair on his head is considered bald.
2. If a man that has one hair on his head is considered bald, then a man that has two hairs on his head is considered bald.
3. If a man that has two hairs on his head is considered bald, then a man that has three hairs on his head is considered bald.

Therefore, a man that has 1,000,000 hairs on his head is considered bald.

Imagine now that we reject one of the other premises besides the first premise. For example, let's imagine the cutoff point to be at 130 hairs. This means that anyone with 129 hairs on his head would be bald, while anyone with 130 hairs on his head would not be bald.

Naturally, many find the epistemic theory to be questionable. If one of the premises is false, how would anyone know which premise it is? Additionally, how would one find out this information? If we use the word *bald*, that word has meaning because of how we use it. But how can we use that word to determine a standard when we can't know what that standard is?

The Truth-Value Gap Theory

Another theory, the truth-value gap theory, states that we cannot know the cutoff point because there is no specific cutoff point. Intuition tells us there exists a group of people for which saying they are bald is simply true, and there exists another group of people for which saying they are bald is simply false. However, there also exists a group of people in the middle. For these people in the middle, calling them bald is not saying anything true or false. For these people, the word *bald* is undefined.

According to the truth-value gap theory, because sentences can be undefined instead of true, not all of the premises are true. However, even the truth-value gap theory runs into problems.

If you were to look at the sentence "It is either raining or not raining," normally you would consider this to be a logical truth. However, under the truth-value gap theory, if there were a borderline case of rain, both "It is raining" and "It is not raining" would be undefined, and therefore neither would be true.

Supervaluationism

Supervaluationism attempts to solve the problem of the middle group discussed in the truth-value gap theory. When looking at the baldness example, there are examples of thinly haired men for whom it would not be true to say that they are bald (as dictated by the rules of being "bald"); however, it would not be false to say they are bald, either. Therefore, it seems to be up to us to determine these cases.

In supervaluationism, drawing the line between baldness and non-baldness is referred to as a "sharpening" of the term *bald*. While simple sentences regarding borderline scenarios can lack a truth-value, compounds of these sentences will in fact have truth-values, and supervaluationism will allow for standard logic to be retained (even with the existence of truth-value gaps). With this idea of sharpening, supervaluationism states the following:

- A sentence is true if and only if it is true with regard to all sharpenings.
- A sentence is false if and only if it is false with regard to all sharpenings.
- A sentence is undefined if and only if it is true with regard to some sharpenings and false with regard to other sharpenings.

So according to supervaluationism, premises of the sorites paradox will be true regarding some sharpenings, false regarding other sharpenings, and therefore, some will be undefined. This allows for there to be valid reasoning with a false conclusion.

However, even supervaluationism has its problems as a theory. Supervaluationism states "It is either raining or not raining" is always true even if neither event is true. If we return to the idea of baldness, supervaluationism would assert that the statement "If you have 130 hairs on your head, you are not bald, but if you have one less, you are bald" is false, while also claiming "There is a number of hairs with which you are not bald, and if you have one less, you are bald" is true. There is clearly a contradiction here.

Denying the Validity of the Sorites Paradox

The third option in attempting to solve the sorites paradox states that one can accept all of the premises but deny the conclusion. According to this option, sentences are not considered to be absolutely true or false; instead, they are considered to be true to a certain degree. Therefore, each statement should be determined by the degrees of truth within its parts.

Accepting the Sorites Paradox as Sound

The last option is to embrace the sorites paradox and accept it as sound. If one embraces the sorites paradox, then it seems that both positive and negative versions must be accepted. No one is bald and everyone is bald. Any number of grains will make a heap and no number of grains can make a heap. Since this cannot be the case, however, embracing the sorites paradox must be more restricted by accepting classical reasoning and denying terms like *baldness* or *heapness*, so that these words apply to nothing.

LUDWIG WITTGENSTEIN (1889–1951)

The anti-systematic philosopher

Ludwig Wittgenstein is considered to be one of the most important philosophers of the twentieth century, and his influence is particularly significant in analytic philosophy. Wittgenstein was born on April 26, 1889, in Vienna, Austria, to one of Austria's richest families. In 1908, Wittgenstein attended Manchester University to study aeronautical engineering, and he soon became extremely interested in the work of Gottlob Frege and the philosophy of mathematics.

From 1911 to 1913, based on the advice of Frege, Wittgenstein studied at Cambridge under Bertrand Russell. At Cambridge, Wittgenstein and Frege worked together on understanding the foundations of logic. Periodically, Wittgenstein would leave for Norway, where he would stay for months at a time and attempt to solve the problems they had discussed. At the start of World War I in 1914, Wittgenstein joined the Austrian army. In 1917, he was captured and spent the remainder of the war as a prisoner of war. During his time at war, Wittgenstein began to write one of his most important philosophical works, *Tractatus Logico-Philosophicus*, which was published in both German and English after the war. This would eventually become known as "early Wittgenstein."

By 1920, Wittgenstein had stopped pursuing philosophy, believing that his work in *Tractatus* had solved all of philosophy's problems. He gave his share of his family's fortune away to his siblings, and for the next nine years, he tried several different professions in Vienna. In 1929, after talking to members of the Vienna Circle about the philosophy of math and science, Wittgenstein decided to return to Cambridge and study philosophy. His return to Cambridge marked a dramatic shift in his philosophy, and the various lectures, conversations, and letters from this time are sometimes referred to as "middle Wittgenstein." It is during this "middle" phase that Wittgenstein rejects dogmatic philosophy (which included not only traditional philosophical works, but also the ideas put forth in his own book).

Wittgenstein spent the 1930s and 1940s conducting seminars at Cambridge. During this time period (referred to as "later Wittgenstein"), Wittgenstein developed his most significant works, which included revolutionary ideas regarding a shift from formal logic to ordinary language, a skepticism toward the pretensions of philosophy, and reflections on mathematics and psychology. Though he had planned to put all of his ideas into a second book entitled *Philosophical Investigations*, in 1945, while preparing the final manuscript, he withdrew the book from publication (but allowed for it to be published posthumously). Wittgenstein spent the next few years traveling and further developing his philosophy until his death in 1951.

EARLY WITTGENSTEIN

The philosophy of early Wittgenstein is based on his book, *Tractatus Logico-Philosophicus*. Wittgenstein draws heavily from the work of Bertrand Russell and Gottlob Frege, and opposes Russell's and Frege's universalist view of logic, in which logic is the ultimate set of laws and is the foundation upon which knowledge is built.

There are seven basic propositions in *Tractatus Logico-Philosophicus*, as translated by D. F. Pears and B. F. McGuinness:

1. The world is all that is the case.
2. What is the case—a fact—is the existence of states of affairs.
3. A logical picture of facts is a thought.
4. A thought is a proposition with sense.
5. A proposition is a truth-function of elementary propositions (an elementary proposition is a truth-function of itself).
6. The general form of a truth-function is $[\bar{p}, \bar{\xi}, N(\bar{\xi})]$.
7. What we cannot speak about we must pass over in silence.

Essentially, Wittgenstein argues that logic has no laws, and cannot be a set of laws, because logic is something completely different from the sciences. The very assumption that logic has laws is the result of assuming that logic is a science, but logic is something else entirely. Logic is strictly form and has no content. While on its own, logic says absolutely nothing, logic is what determines the structure and form of all that is talked about.

Wittgenstein then tackles the role of language. According to Wittgenstein, language is only appropriate to use for describing facts in the world. He argues that language is unsuitable for speaking of things such as value, ideas that relate to something outside of the world, or things that discuss the world in general (thus claiming that a large part of philosophy, including aesthetics, ethics, and metaphysics, cannot be dealt with through language).

For example, one's ethical view is the result of the way in which one views the world and lives. So therefore, how could this be put into words and be expressed as a law? Wittgenstein asserts that one's ethical view (as well as much of philosophy) is something that can only be shown and not stated. He then redefines the purpose of philosophy and states that philosophy is not a doctrine, and therefore, it should not be approached in a dogmatic fashion. The philosopher, according to Wittgenstein, should use logical analysis to show where traditional philosophers went wrong (he refers to all propositions as nonsense) and should correct those who say things that are not sayable. By referring to propositions as nonsense, Wittgenstein even admits that his own book has become dangerously close to nonsense.

LATER WITTGENSTEIN

While Wittgenstein's *Tractatus* claimed philosophy should not be approached dogmatically, Wittgenstein came to the realization that his very own work was dogmatic. Thus, his later works, and particularly his book *Philosophical Investigations*, are most notable for their complete rejection of dogmatism. In doing so, he moves away from logic and toward what he believes should be the foundation of every philosopher, ordinary language. In his book, Wittgenstein details a new way to view language and claims that the purpose of philosophy should be therapeutic.

In discussing the meaning of words, Wittgenstein claims that the meanings of words are determined by how one uses the words, and not by some type of abstract link between reality and language (a drastic change from Wittgenstein's earlier perspective). Meanings of words are not fixed or limited. The meaning of a word can be vague or fluid and still be just as useful.

To support his claims that words are not fixed and have a multitude of uses, Wittgenstein introduces what he calls "language-games" and returns to the idea frequently throughout his book. While he refers to *language-games*, Wittgenstein never fully defines what the term means, so as to further show the fluidity and diversification of language. Though there is no specific or rigid definition, there is no difficulty in understanding the term and using it in the correct way. Thus, Wittgenstein proves that ordinary language is adequate the way it currently stands, and that trying to dig beneath the surface of language results in nothing more than unwarranted generalizations.

A large part of *Philosophical Investigations* pertains to the language of psychology. When we use words like *thinking*, *intending*, *understanding*, and *meaning*, the temptation is to believe that these words indicate our mental processes. By examining how these words are used, Wittgenstein concludes that these words do not refer to a mental state at all; instead, they refer to an individual's behavior.

Wittgenstein comes to see that language and customs are not fixed by laws but by the use of language in social contexts (which Wittgenstein refers to as "forms of life"). Therefore, individuals learn how to use language, at its very core, in social contexts, which is why we are able to understand one another. This is also the reason that it is not possible for one to create his own language to describe inner sensations (for there would be no way of knowing whether a word was used correctly, and thus, the language would be meaningless).

Wittgenstein discusses interpretation through the difference between "seeing that" and "seeing as." Look at the example made famous by Wittgenstein, the "duckrabbit."

"Seeing that" is when something is seen in a straightforward manner (for example, we see that it is a duck), and "seeing as" is when one begins to notice particular aspects (for example, we see it as a rabbit). In seeing something *as* something, we are actually interpreting. We do not interpret the things we see except when we acknowledge that there is more than one interpretation to be had.

While both the early and later work of Wittgenstein support an anti-theoretical stance on what philosophy should and should not be, Wittgenstein dramatically shifts from using logic to prove the impossibility of philosophical theories to encouraging the therapeutic nature of philosophy.

AESTHETICS

Beauty and taste

Aesthetics first began in the eighteenth century and currently consists of two major parts: the philosophy of beauty and the philosophy of taste. While the philosophy of art is indeed a part of aesthetics, aesthetics touches on much more. Not only does aesthetics focus on the value and nature of art; it also involves the reactions to natural objects that then become expressions in language—thus, objects are deemed beautiful or ugly. But these terms are incredibly vague, which leads to the questions: How and why does one consider something to be beautiful or ugly?

TASTE

During the eighteenth century, the concept of taste emerged as a response to the rise of rationalist thought. Instead of the rationalist perspective on beauty, which claimed that we make judgments of beauty through using the principles and concepts of reason, theories of taste began to emerge from British philosophers who mostly worked in empiricism.

Immediacy Thesis

These theories, referred to as the immediacy thesis, claim that judgments of beauty have the immediacy and straightforwardness akin to sensory judgments and are not, or not mainly, brought about by other types of principles. The immediacy thesis states that we do not conclude through reason that something is beautiful; instead, we "taste" that it is beautiful.

While a rationalist might object to this theory by stating that there is a big difference between finding a meal excellent and finding a play to be excellent, the theory of taste states that a play is more complicated, and so it involves more cognitive work, which includes applying various concepts and principles. Therefore, determining the beauty of something like a play is not immediate and cannot be a matter of taste. The theory of beauty is immediate, unlike the earlier ideas that were based on rationalist thought, and that when it comes to judging whether a play is beautiful, it simply cannot be a matter of taste because this action requires more cognitive processes and is not immediate. According to Hume, taste is unlike the five external senses. Rather, taste is an internal sense, meaning it depends upon existing operations in order for beauty to be perceived.

Disinterest

During the time the theory of taste was developed, a popular idea among philosophers was that of egoism, meaning one takes pleasure in an action or trait in order to serve a self-interest. However, those who believed in the theory of taste argued that the resulting pleasure from beauty is actually disinterested, meaning it is not self-interested. People are able to judge something as beautiful or not beautiful without serving their own interests. Philosophers believed that determining virtue works in a similar way. Kant questioned this notion that both virtue and taste are disinterested. Kant's view, which is the current view, was that while taste is disinterested, the pleasure that comes from determining whether an action is morally good must be interested because that judgment represents a desire to perform that action.

THE AESTHETIC

The immediacy thesis and the notion of disinterest relating to beauty can then be applied to "artistic formalism," the idea that the properties that make something art, and determine whether it is good or bad, are formal (meaning they are only capable of being understood through hearing or seeing).

The aesthetic experience can be described as the study of specific states of the mind, such as attitudes, emotions, and responses. In 1757, philosopher Edmund Burke published the famous treatise *On the Sublime and Beautiful*. This piece is one of the most significant written works in aesthetics, and introduces two very important terms (among many) to describe the aesthetic experience: *sublime* and *beautiful*.

Philosophical Definitions

SUBLIME: Judging something as *sublime* originates in one's feelings toward nature, and in the indication of being fragile and alone in this world, which does not belong to us and resists our demands. **BEAUTIFUL:** Judging something as *beautiful* originates in social feelings (particularly romantic feelings), and in one's hope to be comforted through love or desire.

THE PHILOSOPHY OF ART

The philosophy of art plays a key role in aesthetics. There are various elements within the philosophy of art, including the questions of what art is, what should be judged, and what the value of art is.

What Is Art?

How one defines art is a persistent question throughout the philosophy of art, and its meaning constantly evolves. From the days of Plato to around the eighteenth century, a central component to art's definition was the role of representation. However, as romanticism began to grow in the eighteenth and nineteenth centuries, art shifted away from representation and toward expression. As the twentieth century approached, there was yet another shift toward abstraction and appreciating the form. Toward the later decades of the twentieth century, even abstraction was abandoned, and philosophers of art argued that art should not have a tight definition. This idea, known as the "de-definition" of art, was created by philosopher Morris Weitz, who had based his work on that of Wittgenstein.

Judging Art

When you see *Hamlet*, are you judging Shakespeare's manuscript? Are you judging the actors' performance? Do you judge every part of the production, down to the costumes? Are different things judged based on different sets of standards? These questions arise for all types of art—music, painting, drawing, etc.

Value

There are two ways to value art: intrinsically and extrinsically. Those who believe art has an extrinsic value appreciate art as a way to express a recognized moral good and to educate the emotions, while those who believe art has intrinsic value believe that art is valuable in and of itself. According to Leo Tolstoy, who took an extrinsic approach, art's value shared the value of empathy. Others, such as Oscar Wilde, took an intrinsic approach, believing in "art for art's sake."

PHILOSOPHY OF CULTURE

The passing of information

When discussing "culture," philosophers speak of the way in which information is passed on to humans through methods that are not genetic or epigenetic (meaning external things that affect genetics). This idea includes the symbolic and behavioral systems that people use to communicate with one another.

THE IDEA OF CULTURE

Culture did not always have the meaning that we know of today. While the term itself has existed at least since the days of Cicero (106–43 B.C.), *culture* was originally used when discussing the philosophy of education and referred to the educational process a person would go through. Thus, the definition of culture that we know of today is a much newer concept.

Philosophy of Education

Philosophy of education deals with attempting to understand what the proper tools are for people to bestow a part of their culture onto others. When children are born, they are illiterate and without knowledge, and it is from their society and culture that they learn to become a part of that society and culture. Therefore, education remains one of the most important elements of cultural processes.

EXAMPLES OF CULTURAL INFLUENCE

Culture allows people to know and believe in different things, and to have differing tastes. This begs the question of whether or not culture, therefore, can shape normative facts or act as a cover over normative universals. There are many examples of culture that have great influence over us.

Language
Language is cultural (and can differ from culture to culture), and therefore, its effects on thought must be considered cultural effects.

Perceiving and Thinking
Language (which is affected by culture) has great influence over our thought processes, and therefore, it also affects our perception. Cultures can either be based on individualism (such as those found in North America, Western Europe, and the English-speaking Australasia) or collectivism (such as those found in the Middle East, South Asia, East Asia, South America, and the Mediterranean).

Philosophical Definitions

COLLECTIVISM: Individuals see themselves as a part of a collective, and motivations primarily stem from duties to the collective. **INDIVIDUALISM:** Individuals are motivated by their own needs and preferences, and do not see themselves as part of a collective.

Emotions
Emotions are not only fundamental to culture; they are fundamental to being a mammal (dogs, for example, can show joy, sadness, and

fear). Emotions are, therefore, evolved responses that help individuals cope, and must be a part of human nature. Culture can influence how different emotions come about, and sometimes the same action can arouse two completely different emotions depending on the culture. Culture can also influence how emotions are expressed.

Morality

Morality is clearly shaped by culture, and one culture's moral views might be completely different than another culture's. This leads to the idea of cultural relativism.

CULTURAL RELATIVISM

Ethical and moral systems are different for every culture. According to cultural relativism, all of these systems are equally valid, and no system is better than another. The basis of cultural relativism is the notion that no true standards of good and evil actually exist. Therefore, judging whether something is right or wrong is based on individual societies' beliefs, and any moral or ethical opinions are affected by an individual's cultural perspective.

There exists an inherent contradiction in cultural relativism, however. If one embraces the idea that there is no right or wrong, then there exists no way to make judgments in the first place. To deal with this contradiction, cultural relativism creates "tolerance." However, with tolerance comes intolerance, which means that tolerance must imply some sort of ultimate good. Thus, tolerance also goes against the very notion of cultural relativism, and the boundaries of logic make cultural relativism impossible.

EPISTEMOLOGY

The study of knowledge

Epistemology comes from the Greek *episteme*, meaning "knowledge," and *logos*, meaning "study of." Therefore, when talking about epistemology, we are discussing the study of knowledge. Philosophers that study epistemology look at two main categories: the nature of knowledge and the extent of knowledge.

THE NATURE OF KNOWLEDGE

By determining the nature of knowledge, philosophers look at what it means to say you know or don't know something. In order to understand this, one must first comprehend what knowledge is and how to then distinguish between knowing something and not knowing something.

THE EXTENT OF KNOWLEDGE

In order to determine the extent of knowledge, philosophers attempt to understand how much we can and do know and how knowledge is acquired (through things like our senses, reason, and the influence of other people). Epistemology also looks at whether or not our knowledge has a limit and whether there are things that are simply unknowable. Can it be possible that we don't know as much as we believe we know?

TYPES OF KNOWLEDGE

While the word *know* can be used in many ways in language, when philosophers describe knowledge, they claim knowledge is factive, meaning one can only know something if that is the case. With this notion in place, there are several different types of knowledge that philosophers distinguish between:

Procedural Knowledge

Sometimes referred to as "know-how" or competence, procedural knowledge is the knowledge a person has through performing some kind of task or procedure (for example, knowing how to ride a bike).

Acquaintance Knowledge

Acquaintance knowledge, also known as familiarity, is the knowledge attained through experience with something. The information from acquaintance knowledge is only sense-data because another object can never be truly known by a person.

Propositional Knowledge

Propositional knowledge is what epistemologists tend to focus on more than procedural or acquaintance knowledge. Propositions are declarative statements that appear to describe states of affairs or facts (though the proposition can be true or false). For example, both "whales are mammals" and "5 + 5 = 13" are propositions, even though "5 + 5 = 13" is not correct. Propositional knowledge is also known as "knowledge-that," where statements are described through the use of "that-clauses." For example, "He knows *that* the clothing store is in the mall," or "He does not know *that* Albany is the capital of New York."

Propositional knowledge involves knowledge of many different subject matters, including mathematical knowledge, geographical knowledge, scientific knowledge, etc. Therefore, any truth can be known (though there may exist truths that are simply unknowable). One purpose of epistemology is to understand the principles of knowledge so that one can determine what can be known and what cannot be known (this is part of meta-epistemology, which attempts to understand what we can know pertaining to knowledge). Propositional knowledge can also be broken up into *a priori* knowledge (knowledge prior to any experience) and *a posteriori* knowledge (knowledge after an experience).

WHAT IT MEANS TO KNOW SOMETHING

In discussing propositional knowledge, philosophers begin to ask many questions about knowledge, such as what it means to actually know something, what the difference is between knowing something and not knowing something, and what the difference is between a person who knows something and another person who does not know that same something. Since knowledge has a wide range, epistemologists attempt to find an understanding of knowledge that is universal and can be applied to all propositions. There are three agreed-upon requirements: belief, truth, and justification. While these notions were touched upon in the segment discussing the Gettier problem, we will now look at them in greater detail.

As the Gettier problem, there must be a fourth condition, though the details of what this condition entails is still up for debate.

Propositions

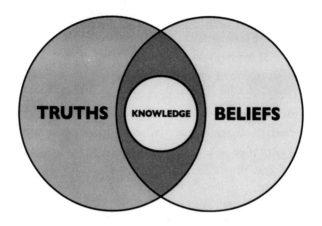

Belief

Knowledge exists solely in the mind and is therefore a mental state. Additionally, knowledge is a type of belief, for if an individual does not have beliefs regarding a certain thing, then there can be no knowledge of that thing. When a belief is actively entertained by an individual, it is known as an occurrent belief. The majority of an individual's beliefs, however, are non-occurrent, meaning the beliefs are not being entertained but are in the background. Similarly, the majority of an individual's knowledge is non-occurrent knowledge, meaning that in a person's mind, only a small portion of knowledge is active.

Truth

Not all beliefs are knowledge. While belief is necessary for knowledge to exist, it is not all that is needed; there needs to be something else that allows for one's thoughts to match up with the real world. When thoughts do not match with the real world, then they cannot be considered knowledge. For example, one cannot know a bridge is safe to cross without first crossing it safely. If you believe the bridge is safe to cross, but as you begin to cross it, it collapses, then you cannot say that you *knew* it was safe. One can believe the bridge is safe to cross, and then only after safely crossing it can one then declare that they *know* it is safe. In the process of acquiring knowledge, people attempt to increase the amount of true beliefs they have (and minimize the amount of false beliefs in the process).

Therefore, for a belief to be deemed knowledge, it must be true. Truth, then, is considered to be a condition of knowledge—if truth did not exist, then neither would knowledge. Even in situations where truth does exist, if there is no truth within a specific domain, then there is no knowledge in that specific domain. For example, if it is true that beauty is in the eye of the beholder, then determining whether something is beautiful cannot be considered knowledge because that belief cannot be true or false. Therefore, knowledge not only requires belief, but factual belief.

Justification

Even when one has factual beliefs, he still does not have knowledge. In order for there to be knowledge, there must be justification of these true beliefs. This means that in order to acquire knowledge, a true belief must have sound reasoning and solid evidence to support its claims. Guessing, faulty reasoning, and misinformation, therefore, cannot be considered knowledge (even if the results are that of the true belief).

While justification is important, it does not imply absolute certainty is needed for there to be knowledge of something. Humans, after all, are fallible, which leads to the notion of fallibility.

Philosophical Definitions

FALLIBILITY: The philosophical idea that no belief can ever truly be supported and justified. This is not to say that there is no such thing as knowledge; rather, this idea claims that even if an individual's true belief is false, it is still possible to have knowledge.

As evidenced by the Gettier problem, the idea of knowledge becomes problematic. We run into further problems when discussing the idea of justification. In thinking about how justification is construed, philosophers discuss two major approaches: internalism and externalism.

Internalism

Internalism is the idea that since beliefs and the forming of beliefs are mental processes, justification depends entirely on internal factors. According to this theory, an individual's other mental states are the only factors involved in determining the justification of a belief.

Externalism

Some claim that if one only focuses on internal factors, beliefs will be mistakenly justified and luck will occur. Externalism claims that there must be at least some external factors that help determine whether or not a belief is justified. The most popular form of externalism, reliabilism, states that the source of beliefs should be taken under consideration. The source can come from a variety of things, like testimony, reason, sense experience, or memory. According to reliabilism, a belief can be justified if it comes from a reliable source.

TWIN EARTH

Taking meaning out of the head

Imagine the following scenario:

There is an imaginary planet, known as Twin Earth, that is absolutely identical to planet Earth down to the smallest detail, with even the inhabitants on both planets being the same. However, there is one difference between Earth and Twin Earth: Wherever there is water on Earth, Twin Earth has a substance, known as XYZ, in those places. For the purposes of this story, this is Earth circa 1750, before the discovery of H_2O (the chemical makeup of water). On this imaginary planet, instead of water in rain, lakes, and oceans, it is the substance XYZ. Furthermore, XYZ has similar observable properties to water, but it has a different microstructure. Inhabitants of Twin Earth (who refer to their own planet as Earth), who are identical to the inhabitants of Earth, speak their own "English" and refer to XYZ as "water."

Now, when Oscar, an inhabitant of Earth, and his twin, an inhabitant of Twin Earth (also named Oscar), say the word *water*, do they mean the same thing?

According to philosopher (and creator of the Twin Earth thought experiment) Hilary Putnam, Oscar and Twin-Oscar do not mean the same thing because while Oscar is referring to H_2O, Twin-Oscar is referencing XYZ. From this, Putnam concludes that the mental processes from the brain cannot suffice in determining what a term references and that one has to understand the causal history that led to the meaning of that term being acquired.

Putnam's Twin Earth thought experiment is one of the most popular examples of his theory in philosophy of language known as "semantic externalism."

SEMANTIC EXTERNALISM

Hilary Putnam attempts to understand how syntax, the arrangement of words, gains meaning (semantics). According to Putnam's semantic externalism, the meaning of a word is determined (either partially or entirely) by factors that are external to the speaking individual. While other theories believed the process of gaining meaning was internal (within the head), Putnam's semantic externalism claimed that the process of gaining semantics is outside the head. In other words, as Putnam famously stated, " 'meanings' just ain't in the head!"

According to Putnam, the meaning of any term in a language consists of a specific sequence of elements:

1. The object that the term is referring to (in the case of Twin Earth, this is the substance with the chemical makeup of H_2O).
2. The typical terms (known as "stereotypes") that are often associated with the term (like the terms *odorless*, *colorless*, and *hydrating* that water is often associated with).

3. The semantic indicators that categorize the object (like *liquid*).

4. The syntactic indicators (for example, a mass noun—a type of noun that has terms being referred to that are not considered to be separate entities).

Based on his ideas of semantic externalism, Putnam goes on to explain his causal theory of reference. He claims that words gain their referents as the result of a chain of causation that ends at the referent. For example, one still has the ability to reference the pyramids in Egypt even if he has never seen them because the concept of what the pyramids are still exists. How can this be? It is because the term has been acquired as a result of interacting with others (who, to acquire their knowledge, had interacted with others, who had acquired their knowledge by interacting with others, etc.). This pattern continues until it eventually reaches a person who had firsthand experience with the subject matter. Because of this chain of causation, one is able to discuss something without ever having experienced it firsthand.

NARROW MENTAL CONTENT

Hilary Putnam's thought experiment, Twin Earth, is part of a bigger topic of discussion known as "broad content," which is the opposing viewpoint of "narrow mental content." The idea behind narrow mental content is that mental content is internal (or intrinsic), and therefore, unlike Putnam's semantic externalism, it does not depend on one's environment at all; rather, it is a property that is intrinsic to that particular thing. (For example, an intrinsic property of a penny is that it is round, while a penny being in someone's pocket is an extrinsic property.) The narrow content of one's belief about an object has to be shared by every duplicate of that individual object.

Some who believe narrow mental content to be true claim that mental content and behavior are the results of a causal consequence from our beliefs. In other words, we act the way we do because of our beliefs and desires. Others claim that people have introspective access to their thoughts, meaning we should have the ability to determine whether the same content is contained in two of our thoughts. According to this claim, the two Oscars, unaware of the chemical makeup of H_2O and XYZ, have no way of knowing whether their thoughts are H_2O-related thoughts or XYZ-related thoughts because they are not even aware the other water-like substance even exists. To make sense of this, philosophers created the notion of "slow-switching." What if Oscar were to move to Twin Earth? At first, he will continue to have water-thoughts about this substance, but the longer he interacts with XYZ and the longer he is away from H_2O, he will come to just think of XYZ and not about H_2O. Over time, his water-thoughts will have a different broad content (and Oscar would not be aware of this change because his thoughts would seem to have the same content as it always did). In order to have introspective access and see that these contents are different, we need narrow mental content and not broad content.

Narrow mental content is controversial to philosophers; many reject it in favor of broad mental content. Putnam's Twin Earth is the most famous example of why broad mental content makes more sense. Both Oscars have the exact same intrinsic properties; however, they are referring to different substances. Therefore, intrinsic properties are not enough to determine what the Oscars are referring to. And this brings us back to Putnam's famous quote, " 'meanings' just ain't in the head!"

ARTHUR SCHOPENHAUER (1788–1860)

The pessimistic philosopher

Arthur Schopenhauer was born on February 22, 1788, in Danzig (present-day Gdansk), Poland. When Schopenhauer was a young man, his father, a merchant, offered the academically inclined Arthur a proposition: he could either prepare to go to a university, or he could travel across Europe with his parents and then take an apprenticeship with a merchant upon returning from their travels. Schopenhauer chose to travel with his family, and on this journey he witnessed firsthand the terrible suffering of the poor throughout Europe. This experience would greatly influence the pessimistic worldview he would later become known for as a philosopher.

Upon returning from his trip across Europe, Schopenhauer began to prepare for his career by holding up his end of the bargain and becoming an apprentice for a merchant. When Schopenhauer was just seventeen years old, his father died (in what is believed to have been a suicide), and two years later, Schopenhauer left the apprenticeship and pursued his academic career.

While Schopenhauer attended school, his mother, who had moved to Weimar, started to become frequently engaged in intellectual and social circles. As she worked as a writer and hostess for a salon that was frequented by many influential thinkers of the time, she introduced her son to Johann Wolfgang von Goethe (with whom he would eventually write a theory on colors) and Friedrich Majer (who sparked Schopenhauer's interest in Eastern thought).

Schopenhauer's relationship with his mother would grow to become so tense that when he was thirty years old, his mother told him to never talk to her again.

By 1809, now attending the University of Göttingen, Schopenhauer had studied medicine until his third semester, when he decided to shift to philosophy. Schopenhauer would eventually transfer to the University of Berlin to continue his philosophical studies. In 1813, due to the onslaught of Napoleon's Grande Armée, Schopenhauer fled to the small town of Rudolstadt, where he would go on to write *The Fourfold Root of the Principle of Sufficient Reason*, an investigation into the idea of sufficient reason. By the next year, Schopenhauer had moved to Dresden, where he would write his famous color theory, *On Vision and Colors*, and an overview of his philosophical system, *The World as Will and Representation*.

By 1820, Schopenhauer had become a lecturer at the University of Berlin. He became extremely competitive with fellow lecturer Wilhelm Hegel, often scheduling his lectures at the same time as Hegel's in order to make audiences choose one over the other. But while Hegel's lectures were crowded with students, Schopenhauer's lectures had very few, and Schopenhauer grew cynical and felt alienated from the academic world. It was only in his later years that his work finally gained traction and became fashionable throughout Europe.

THE PHILOSOPHIES OF SCHOPENHAUER

While the philosophical work of Arthur Schopenhauer touched on a variety of subjects, generally speaking, there is always a theme of pessimism and the presence of pain within the human condition.

The Fourfold Root of the Principle of Sufficient Reason

In his published dissertation of 1813, Schopenhauer looks at the assumption among philosophers that the universe is understandable, and criticizes the principle of sufficient reason, which states that things that are real are rational. Schopenhauer stated that in order to use the principle of sufficient reason, one has to be able to think of something that would then need to be explained, which means there must be the presence of a subject to begin with. Thus, the perceiving mind is the only thing that makes experiences possible. He concludes that the world, therefore, is just a representation.

Philosophy of the "Will"

Perhaps Schopenhauer's most significant philosophical work was on individual motivation. Schopenhauer criticized the optimism in the theories of Kant and Hegel, which claimed that society and reason determine one's individual morality. Instead, Schopenhauer claimed that individuals are motivated by their own desires, or "will to live," that can never be satisfied, and that this is what guides humanity. It is here that we see Schopenhauer's commitment to pessimism and view of humanity in a negative light, which persists throughout the body of his work. The "Will," according to Schopenhauer, brings about all of mankind's suffering, and this suffering is the result of constantly desiring more.

Schopenhauer concluded that human desire (and therefore human action) has no direction or logic and is futile. He claimed that the world is not only a terrible place (with things like cruelty, disease, suffering, etc.); it is the worst of worlds, and if it could be even slightly worse, it would cease to exist.

Aesthetics

According to Schopenhauer, aesthetics separates intellect from the Will and is not linked to the body. He considered art to be either an act that is predetermined in the mind of the artist before the artist creates anything or an act that is spontaneous, while the body is nothing more than just an extended part of the Will.

If the Will that guides humans is based on desire, art allows one to temporarily escape the pain of the world because aesthetic contemplation makes an individual stop perceiving the world as just presentation. Art, therefore, goes beyond sufficient reason. To Schopenhauer, music is the purest form of art because he believed it has the ability to embody the Will.

Ethics

In Schopenhauer's moral theory, he identified three primary incentives that guide morality in humans: egoism, malice, and compassion.

- **Egoism:** This is responsible for guiding humanity to perform actions that are self-interested and makes one desire pleasure and happiness. Schopenhauer believed that the majority of human deeds stem from egoism.
- **Malice:** Schopenhauer distinguishes between acts of egoism and acts of malice, which are independent of personal gain and are performed with the intention to harm others.
- **Compassion:** This, according to Schopenhauer, is the only genuine thing that can drive moral acts, for only the good of an act is sought out, and cannot occur from a sense of duty or personal benefit.

Schopenhauer also viewed love as an unconscious element that helps the "will-to-live," a force that makes man desire to reproduce and therefore continue to exist.

Eastern Philosophy

Schopenhauer is notable for being one of the first philosophers to incorporate Eastern thought into his work, and he was particularly drawn to Hindu and Buddhist philosophy. His pessimistic viewpoint is incredibly influenced by the Four Noble Truths found in Buddhism, and indeed, he used them as a foundation to build his pessimistic theory.

THE FOUR NOBLE TRUTHS	SCHOPENHAUER'S ADDITIONS
1. Life means suffering.	The world is Vorstellung
2. The root of suffering is desire.	a. The cause of suffering is willing. b. The world as Der Wille
3. There is hope.	There is little hope.
4. Hope is found within the Noble Eightfold Path.	Hope is found in: a. Aesthetic contemplation b. The practice of aestheticism

Schopenhauer claims the world is *Vorstellung*, meaning "representation." So not only is life full of suffering; the world is not completely real and is just a representation of reality (much like Plato's cave). *Der Wille* is the Will, and it is beneath the surface appearance of everything.

Schopenhauer also drew upon the holy writings of Hinduism, the Upanishads, when formulating the central idea to his philosophy: that the world is the expression of the Will.

KARL MARX (1818–1883)

The father of communism

Karl Marx was born on May 5, 1818, in Prussia. Marx's father was a successful lawyer involved in the Prussian reform movement, and valued the work of Voltaire and Kant. Though both of Kant's parents were Jewish, his father converted to Lutheranism as the result of an 1815 law that banned Jews from having full citizenship rights.

Karl Marx attended the University of Bonn in 1835, before transferring to the University of Berlin at the request of his father (who considered it to be a more serious school). At the University of Berlin, Marx started studying law before switching to philosophy, and began to learn the work of Hegel. Soon, Marx would become part of a radical group of students known as the Young Hegelians, who criticized the religious and political establishments of the time.

In 1841, Marx earned his doctorate from the University of Jena, where he wrote his dissertation on ancient Greek natural philosophy. He was denied a teaching position because of his radical political ideologies. Marx then began working as a journalist, and became editor of the liberal newspaper *Rheinische Zeitung* in 1842. Only one year later, however, the government shut down the paper. Marx then married and moved to Paris, where, in 1844, he would collaborate with Friedrich Engels in writing a criticism of Bruno Bauer (a former friend and Young Hegelian). Marx was soon expelled from France for once again writing for another radical newspaper (this newspaper had close ties to an organization that would eventually turn into the Communist League), so he moved to Brussels.

During his time in Brussels, Karl Marx broke away from the ideology of the Young Hegelians upon being introduced to the ideas of socialism. While living in Brussels, Marx developed his theory of historical materialism that would appear in his *The German Ideology* and wrote *Theses on Feuerbach* (which would not be published until after his death because he could not find a publisher willing to publish the books).

In 1846, in an attempt to connect socialists across Europe, Marx created a Communist Correspondence Committee. The ideas set forth by Marx inspired socialists in England to form the Communist League, and in 1847, at the request of the Central Committee that was meeting in London, Marx and Engels wrote *Manifest der Kommunistischen Partei* (commonly known as *The Communist Manifesto*). *The Communist Manifesto* was published in 1848, and as a result, Karl Marx was expelled from Belgium in 1849. After being deported from France and refused renaturalization by Prussia, Marx eventually ended up in London, where he participated in the development of the German Workers' Educational Society and created the new headquarters for the Communist League. In 1867, Marx published the first volume of his treatise on economics, *Das Kapital*, which is considered to be his greatest achievement. Marx spent the remainder of his life working on the manuscripts for the next two volumes; however, he died before their completion, and the books were subsequently published after his death.

THE PHILOSOPHICAL THEMES OF KARL MARX

Marx's canon of work focuses on the individual's role as a laborer and his connection to the exchange of goods and services.

Historical Materialism

Marx was incredibly influenced by the philosophical work of Hegel; particularly, Hegel's belief that human consciousness had evolved from simple efforts in understanding objects to self-awareness and other higher, more complex and abstract thought processes. Hegel claimed that history, too, had a similar dialectical view; contradictions of a specific time period lead to a newer time period attempting to smooth over those previous contradictions.

While Marx agreed with much of Hegel's view on history, Hegel was an idealist and Marx considered himself to be a materialist. So while Hegel believed that ideas are the primary way in which people relate to their surroundings and that one is able to understand history based on ideas that are representative of that time period, Marx believed that the ways societies are organized during a time period in history is actually the fundamental truth regarding that society. Marx viewed history as an evolving pattern of a series of economic systems that lead to the creation of different societies through bringing about feelings of resentment among classes.

Alienation of Labor

Marx argues that a key component to one's sense of well-being and conception of self is labor. When one works on turning objective matter into something of sustenance and value, one views himself as externalized and as if he has met the requirements of existence. Marx claimed that labor is not only an act of personal creation; it is a display of one's identity and survival.

Marx states that the worker under capitalism, however, with it being a system based on private ownership, takes away the self-worth and identity that is essential to the worker. The worker, now distant from the product, becomes alienated from his work, himself, and his coworkers. There is no longer a personal sense of satisfaction for the worker, and he now views his work as simply a way to survive. Because the worker is estranged from the work process and since labor is a key component to one's self, the worker must also be estranged from his self and from humanity as a whole. The constant alienation that is formed by capitalism thus creates the antagonistic relationship discussed in historical materialism, and will eventually lead to the destruction of capitalism.

The Labor Theory of Value

Marx states that the meaning of the term *commodity* is "an external object that fulfills needs or wants." He also makes a distinction between use-value (the capacity to fulfill such needs or wants) and exchange-value (the value—measured in money—relating to other commodities). All commodities are the products of labor, and according to Karl Marx, a commodity's value should not be determined by something like supply and demand; rather, its value should be based on the amount of labor that went into creating that commodity. Therefore, a commodity's value in the market should be representative of the labor and production that went into it.

Labor Theory of Value

Marx's labor theory of value is significant because it would become the root of his theory of exploitation, which states that profit is the result of employers exploiting their workers.

In order for a person to satisfy his own needs and wants through the purchase of commodities, he must first produce and sell a commodity of his own, and such transactions can only occur through the use of money. Marx argued that motivation among capitalists is driven not by a desire for commodities, but by a desire for money. This idea is then taken advantage of, and capitalists create wages and working hours to get the most labor with the least cost, and then sell for more than they paid, not by the commodity's exchange-value. By creating what Marx refers to as a "surplus value," capitalists exploit workers.

Mode of Production and Relations of Production

According to Marx, a society's organization of economic production is known as a "mode of production." Within the mode of production is the "means of production," which is used by a society to create goods (for example, raw materials, factories, machines, and even the labor). Marx then describes the "relations of production" as the relationships between those who do not own the means of production (like the workers) and those who do (like the bourgeoisie or capitalists). Karl Marx claimed that history's evolution is the result of the mode of production interacting with the relations of production. As the mode of production continues to evolve to the fullest productive capacity, hostility among classes in accordance with the relations of production begins to form (in other words, it becomes the owners versus the workers).

The mode of production known as capitalism, according to Marx, is based on the fact that the means of production is based on private ownership. Capitalism is based on the idea of getting the most out of labor for the lowest cost, and workers are only paid enough so that they can be kept alive and can continue to produce. Marx claims that the workers will come to understand the exploitation and antagonistic nature of capitalism, and that this will ultimately lead to the overthrow of capitalism by the working class. In replacement of capitalism, the new mode of production will be based on a means of production involving collective ownership; and this is communism.

The Marxist Conception of Society

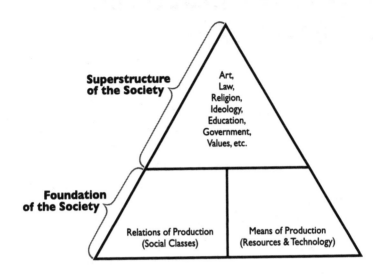

Commodity Fetishism

Marx believed that as people attempt to understand the world, they become fixated on things like money (how to get it, who has it, how to spend it, etc.) and commodities (the costs of buying or making a product, the demand of a product, etc.). These were viewed by Marx as "fetishes," things that people fixate on that, in turn, prevent people from understanding the truth. These fetishes are what prevent people from understanding the truth regarding the exploitation of the working class. Thus, in capitalism, the market price of a commodity in everyday life not only depends upon exploitation; it also masks the exploitation of workers. Therefore, Marx claimed, the presence of commodity fetishism is what allows the capitalist mode of production to continue without having to confront the exploitation that it causes.

MARTIN HEIDEGGER (1889–1976)

Being and Time

Martin Heidegger was born on September 26, 1889, in Messkirch, Germany. Messkirch was a rural town that was deeply conservative and religious, and this upbringing would have a profound impact on Heidegger's philosophical career. In 1909, Heidegger began studying theology at the University of Freiburg, but by 1911, he had shifted his focus toward philosophy.

Though incredibly influenced by many philosophers, the impact of Aristotle's *Metaphysics*, and particularly Aristotle's desire to understand what unites the different modes of being, would have a profound effect on Heidegger. This, along with the work of Edmund Husserl, whom Heidegger worked for as an assistant in 1919 and whose chair he would take over when Husserl retired, led him to his most famous work: *Being and Time.*

Being and Time was published in 1927 and was praised for being an incredibly significant text of continental philosophy. It is still considered to be one of the single most important works of the twentieth century, and is viewed as an impetus for many of the greatest philosophical thinkers.

Following the publication of *Being and Time*, there was a noticeable shift in Heidegger's philosophy, which Heidegger referred to as "the turn." To Heidegger, the turn was not a shift in his thinking, but rather a shift in Being. Heidegger described the elements of the turn in what is considered to be his second most important work,

Contributions to Philosophy, which was not published in German until 1989, even though it was written around 1936.

Heidegger became a member of the Nazi Party in 1933 and was elected rector of Freiburg University. While accounts of his time as rector vary—some say he enthusiastically brought Nazi policy into the university education, while others claim he allowed the implementation of policy while holding an underground resistance movement toward some of the details of the Nazi policy (such as anti-Semitism)—Heidegger was not rector for long, resigning from the position in 1934. That same year, Heidegger began to grow distant from the Nazi Party, even though he never officially left it. When World War II ended, the University of Freiburg's denazification committee investigated Heidegger and banned him from teaching. The ban would last until 1949, when the following year he would become professor emeritus.

BEING AND TIME

Being and Time is Martin Heidegger's most important and complex philosophical work, and it skyrocketed Heidegger into becoming one of the most significant philosophers of the twentieth century.

Heidegger examined the metaphysical question of what it means to be "being." He begins by looking at the work of Descartes, who claimed that *being* is divided into three different types of substances:

1. Entities that do not need other entities
2. *Res cogitans* (nonmaterial substances)
3. *Res extensa* (material substances)

According to Heidegger, this idea of Being leads to "indefinite difference" because there is the assumption that Being can exist in all three of these possibilities, and that simply does not make sense. Secondly, Heidegger concluded that Descartes's belief of Being is incorrect, for Descartes's findings simply show the world to be made up of res extensa and that Being simply means "knowing another object."

Heidegger, on the other hand, believed the best way to understand Being is by looking internally and interrogating our own selves. Therefore, he concluded, the Being is us. He referred to this as Dasein, meaning "Being-there," and this, according to Heidegger, is Being asking itself the question of what Being is. Therefore, Dasein is a self-interpreting Being, one that says "I," and one that has a "mineness." Self-interpretation, therefore, is existence.

Heidegger then goes on to clarify that there are three modes of Being:

1. Dasein
2. Presence-at-hand (things that exist by looking, observing something, and only becoming concerned with the bare facts and concepts)
3. Readiness-at-hand (the Being possessed by things like equipment, where not only are they useable; they have always been manipulatable because of their Being)

In Dasein, the normal mode of existence is neither authentic nor inauthentic because it is an average everydayness—it is like life is living a person, and not the person living life.

In Heidegger's opinion, conceptions of the subject are incorrect because the subject becomes converted into an object. Rather, the subject should be seen as "Being-in-the-world." Instead of the environment being filled with objects, it is filled with things. These things are called Zeug, meaning "gear," and are used for accomplishing projects. *Zeug* is only significant or meaningful if it is what it is within the specific project(s) it appears in, or if it is what it is when compared to other things that are part of the project(s). Therefore, *Zeug*'s particular Being is that of readiness-at-hand. A thing's Being is given to it, as that thing, through the context of a project of *Dasein* and the context of other things involved in that project. In other words, things already are what they are due to their place in reference to other things.

Dasein cannot make meaning, however, for it is not a unitary entity that is completely self-present. The individuality of *Dasein* creates a unique, but flawed, perspective, because it is always in relation to other things and always in a world inhabited by other things. The gear (like language, projects, and words) is not for one person alone, so therefore *Dasein* is what Heidegger refers to as "they-self."

Heidegger concludes that the Being of *Dasein* is time. While, as a mortal, *Dasein* runs from birth until death, *Dasein*'s access to the world is through tradition and history.

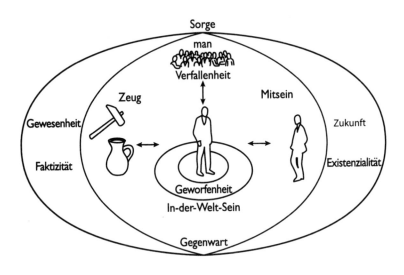

From left to right: *Gewesenheit* means "living past" or "been-ness." *Faktizität* means "thrown-ness" because, according to Heidegger, people are thrown into the world. *Zeug* means "equipment" and is the object that one has meaningful dealings with. *Sorge* means "care" or "concern," which, according to Heidegger, is the fundamental basis of one's being-in-the-world because it creates drive in us. *Verfallenheit* means "fallen" or "estranged." *Geworfenheit* means "being thrown." *In-der-Welt-Sein* means "Being-in-the-world." *Gegenwart* means "present." *Mitsein* means "Being-with." *Zukunft* means "future." *Existenzialität* means "existentiality."

THE TURN

Sometime after World War II, Heidegger's work began to shift focus. Heidegger began focusing on how behavior on its own is dependent upon an already existing "openness to being." Heidegger stated that the maintenance of this prior openness is the essence of being human, and claimed that the modern human is forgetting about this openness. According to Heidegger, this type of openness was authentic during the days of pre-Socratic philosophers like Heraclitus and Anaximander; however, it started to become forgotten with the philosophical works of Plato.

Heidegger also became interested in technology and poetry, believing that both are contrasting methods of "revealing" Being. While the creation of new poetry has the ability to reveal Being, new technology "frames" existence (his notion known of *Gestell*) and further reveals the distinction between subject and object. Heidegger said that while technology may play a role in allowing humans to have a new understanding of their Being, the framing that technology has created threatens mankind's ability to reveal and experience the more primal truth.

VOLTAIRE (1694–1778)

The controversial philosopher

François-Marie d'Arouet (who would later go by the name Voltaire) was born on November 21, 1694, in Paris, France. Voltaire is considered to be one of the single most important philosophers of the Enlightenment era. The work Voltaire produced during his lifetime was so varied that it can be hard to classify him as a philosopher in the traditional sense. Besides philosophy, Voltaire also wrote plays, novels, historical pieces, poetry, essays, and scientific texts.

Voltaire was born into a middle-class family; his mother came from a noble family, and his father was a minor treasury official and notary. At the age of seven, Voltaire's mother passed away, and Voltaire became close with his godfather, Chateauneuf, a freethinker who would have an immense impact on his life and teach the young Voltaire about literature, deism, and to renounce superstitions.

From 1704 to 1711, Voltaire attended the Collège Louis-le-Grand in Paris, where he received a classical education and was adept at learning languages (while he had already learned Greek and Latin when he was younger, he later also became fluent in English, Spanish, and Italian). When he finished his studies, he had already made his mind up about wanting to be a writer. His father, however, wanted his son to be a lawyer, believing writers contributed nothing of value to society, and so Voltaire lied to his father about being an assistant to a lawyer while he composed his satirical poetry. Eventually, Voltaire's father found out and sent his son to law school, but Voltaire continued to pursue his passion, and he began circulating in intellectual circles.

Voltaire's Trouble with French Authority

Throughout his life, Voltaire had a history of opposing French authority and, as a result, faced several imprisonments and exiles. In 1717, while still in his twenties, Voltaire was imprisoned for eleven months at the infamous Bastille prison for writing defamatory poetry about the regent for King Louis XV. During his stay at the Bastille, he wrote his first play, *Oedipe*, which became a success, and by 1718, he had taken on the name "Voltaire" (which was a play on words), and this is often considered the point at which he formally separated from his past.

From 1726 to 1729, after offending a nobleman, Voltaire was forced to live in exile in England. While in England, Voltaire was introduced to the ideas of John Locke, Sir Isaac Newton, and Britain's constitutional monarchy, which embraced freedom of religion and freedom of speech. Upon returning to Paris, Voltaire wrote of his experience and views of Britain and published *Philosophical Letters on the English* in 1733. This was met with an incredible amount of controversy from the French government and church, and Voltaire was once again forced to flee Paris.

Voltaire lived in exile in northeastern France for the next fifteen years with Émilie du Châtelet, his lover and collaborator. He continued to write works in science, history, fiction, and philosophy (particularly in metaphysics, concentrating on the legitimacy of the Bible and the existence of God). Not only did Voltaire call for religious freedom and the separation of church and state; he had renounced religion entirely.

When du Châtelet died in 1749, Voltaire moved to Potsdam to work under Frederick the Great. By 1753, however, Voltaire once again found himself in great controversy when he attacked the

218

PHILOSOPHY 101

president of the Berlin Academy of Sciences. Voltaire then spent a period of time traveling city to city; however, due to his many bans, he eventually ended up close to the Swiss border (it was here that he wrote his famous *Candide*).

At the age of eighty-three, Voltaire finally returned to Paris in 1778, where he received a hero's welcome. He died on May 30 of that same year.

THE PHILOSOPHY OF VOLTAIRE

Voltaire was greatly influenced by John Locke and the skeptical empiricism that was occurring in England at the time. Not only was Voltaire an outspoken critic of religion; he was also responsible for the shift away from the work of Descartes and mocked religious and humanistic forms of optimism.

Religion

Voltaire was a firm believer in religious liberty. Though he was not an atheist (in fact, he thought of himself as a deist), he was opposed to organized religion and Catholicism, and saw the Bible as a metaphorical moral reference that was outdated and created by man. He instead believed that the existence of God is not a matter of faith (and therefore, is not based on a particular faith), but of reason. Voltaire is famous for having said, "If God did not exist, it would be necessary to invent Him."

Politics

Voltaire viewed the French monarchy, and its unfair balance of power, in an incredibly negative light. According to Voltaire, the bourgeoisie was too little and ineffective; the aristocracy was too corrupt and parasitic; the commoners were too superstitious and ignorant; and the only usefulness of the church was to use its religious tax to create a base strong enough to go against the monarchy.

Voltaire believed that the constitutional monarchy that he witnessed in England was the ideal form of government. He did not trust democracy (claiming it to be the "idiocy of the masses") and believed that with the aid of philosophers, an enlightened monarch could improve the wealth and power of France (which, he argued, was in the best interest of the monarch).

Hedonism

Voltaire's views on liberty, and really all of his philosophy, were based on hedonistic morality. This was often expressed in Voltaire's poetry, which presented moral freedom that was attained through sexual liberty. Voltaire's writing presented morality as being rooted in the positive assessment of personal pleasure. His ideas regarding ethics were based on maximizing pleasure while reducing pain. His hedonistic viewpoints even translated into his critique of religion; he frequently attacked the teachings of Catholicism with regard to the moral codes of sexual constraint, priestly celibacy, and bodily abnegation.

Skepticism

Unlike the stances of other philosophers like Descartes (whose work Voltaire detested), Voltaire's entire philosophical stance was based on skepticism. According to Voltaire, other philosophers like Descartes were "philosophical *romanciers*," and he saw no value in creating systematic accounts in order to explain things in some type of coherent way. This type of philosophy, according to Voltaire, was not philosophy at all, but fiction. Voltaire claimed that the role of the philosopher is to understand that sometimes no explanation is the most philosophical explanation. The philosopher should liberate people from their dogmatic principles and irrational laws.

Voltaire used skepticism as a way to defend his ideology on liberty, and claimed that there is no such thing as an authority sacred enough to be immune from criticism. There is a constant hostility in Voltaire's work, be it in his views on the monarchy, religion, or society. He used wit and satire to undermine philosophical standpoints throughout his career. For example, his most famous work, *Candide*, parodied the religious optimism of philosopher Gottfried Leibniz.

Metaphysics

Voltaire claimed that science, due in large part to the significant advances of Sir Isaac Newton (whom Voltaire was a great proponent of), was moving away from metaphysics. Voltaire argued that metaphysics should be eliminated from science entirely, and indeed, he was the most vocal supporter of this notion.

RELATIVISM

Being relative to something else

Relativism is not one specific view in particular, but rather a wide variety of views that share two common themes: thought, evaluation, experience, or reality is in some way relative to something else, and no standpoint is more privileged than another.

Relativistic ideas can be found in almost all areas of philosophical study. Typically, arguments based in relativism start with assertions of plausible arguments that, by the end, result in implausible conclusions. By all accounts, these arguments sound better when thought of in abstract ways (they seem to become flawed and trivial when applied to real situations). It is for this reason that few philosophers defend relativism.

This is not to say that relativism is completely useless, however. In fact, some of the most important philosophers to have ever lived have been associated with (or accused of being) relativists.

THE STRUCTURE OF RELATIVISM

Generally speaking, one can think of relativism as: Y is relative to X.

Here, Y, which is considered to be a dependent variable, can be replaced with different attributes of experience, thought, evaluation, or reality, and X, considered to be an independent variable, can be replaced with something that is believed to contribute to a difference in the value of Y. "Is relative to" represents the type of connection occurring between X and Y.

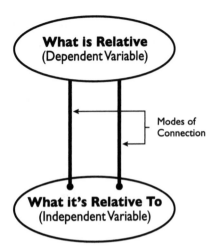

Examples of dependent variables (Y) include perception, reality, truth, practice, central beliefs, central concepts, ethics, and semantics.

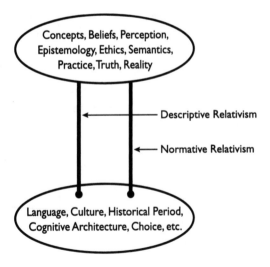

Examples of independent variables (X) include religion, language, historical period, culture, race, gender, and social status.

TYPES OF RELATIVISM

Descriptive Relativism

Descriptive relativism is the belief that different cultures have different moral codes (thoughts, reasoning, etc.). Principles of two groups are not evaluated, and nothing is implied about how one group should act or behave. Rather, the principles of the groups are described. Descriptive relativism, unlike normative relativism, is a theory pertaining to anthropology.

Normative Relativism

Normative relativism is a theory in ethics. It states that people ought to follow the moral code of their society or culture. Therefore, immoral behavior is behavior that goes against the moral code of that specific society or culture. There is no such thing as a universal moral principle, for moral codes of one society, under normative relativism, are no better or worse than those of another society. Lastly, according to normative relativism, there must be a tolerance of other societies' moral codes, meaning it is wrong to judge or force moral beliefs onto another society.

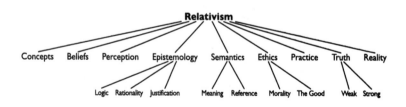

Matters of Degree

Having differences in beliefs, concepts, or epistemic standards does not necessarily mean views are different from one another. In relativism, there are some ideas that are more central than others.

If a feature plays a prominent role in the development of a group's beliefs, it is considered to be a central concept. When philosophers refer to something as a central belief, that means the belief is so critical to a group or individual that if it were to be abandoned, other beliefs would be abandoned as a result. For example, the notion that physical objects still exist even if no one is around to perceive them can be viewed as a central belief, while the idea that kings have the right to rule the land based on divine right is not a lasting belief, and therefore not a central belief. Central concepts and central beliefs are related to one another and often involve each other. With that said, centrality is not black-and-white and often comes in degrees.

Relativism can also be local (applied only to a limited part of the cognitive or evaluative life of an individual or group) or global. However, locality also comes in degrees.

ARGUMENTS SUPPORTING RELATIVISM

Oftentimes, relativism is assumed more than argued for. However, the most common arguments for relativism are the following.

Perception Is Theory-Laden

Perceptual relativism claims that perception (what we see, hear, feel, etc.) with regard to a situation is, in part, the result of the beliefs, expectations, and concepts that we already have. According to perceptual relativism, perception is not considered to be a physiological process that makes all people perceive things in the same way.

While notions that are theory-laden are descriptive with regard to the ways in which perception is described, they alone do not come to any normative conclusions. However, it can be extremely difficult, and even impossible, to strictly follow the scientific idea of perception when observations are clearly colored and affected by our expectations and beliefs.

The most famous hypothetical situation of this is from philosopher N. R. Hanson. Hanson claimed that if, for example, Johannes Kepler (who believed the solar system is heliocentric, meaning the planets revolve around the sun) and Tycho Brahe (who believed in a geocentric solar system, where the sun and moon revolve around Earth and the rest of the planets revolve around the sun) were to both look at the same sunrise, they would think that two completely different things were happening. While Brahe would view the event as the sun rising, Kepler would see it as the sun staying in place, with the horizon dipping away.

Alternative Frameworks Are Incommensurable

An individual's sentences and words (which are representative of his beliefs and concepts) are determined by how one's culture, linguistic community, scientific foundations, etc., shaped that individual. If two of these foundations were incredibly different from one another (for example, one group's scientific foundations drastically differ from another group's culture), then people from the other group would not be able to communicate with people from the first group because the first group's words and sentences would have no meaning to the second group.

If this theory is considered to be sound, perception can then be used to support this claim, for differing foundations will make two groups perceive things differently.

ARGUMENTS AGAINST RELATIVISM

There are many arguments against relativism. Which argument is used depends on whether the subject of debate is descriptive relativism or normative relativism.

Arguments Against Descriptive Relativism
No Concepts or Beliefs Exist in the First Place

Groups cannot have differing concepts or beliefs if there are no concepts or beliefs that exist to begin with. This argument was made by American philosopher Willard van Orman Quine, who claimed that there are no facts. If this is the case, then it also would not make sense to have normative questions pertaining to whether or not a concept or belief is better than another individual or group's.

Perception Is Not Completely Theory-Laden

The theory of descriptive perceptual relativism states that perception may be partially theory-laden; however, it is not as severely theory-laden as those who subscribe to extreme relativism would claim it to be. This theory further weakens the notion that perception is theory-laden because it also shows support for several different forms of normative relativism.

The extent to which our perceptions are influenced by concepts, expectations, and beliefs is still controversial, but most philosophers agree that these factors play a critical role. After all, we still talk of the sun rising and setting. And this is almost four centuries after Kepler's groundbreaking work! Even during the time of Kepler and Brahe, it was understood that, regardless of the scientific reasoning behind the sun rising and setting, both men were seeing the exact same thing.

Brahe's Model of the Solar System

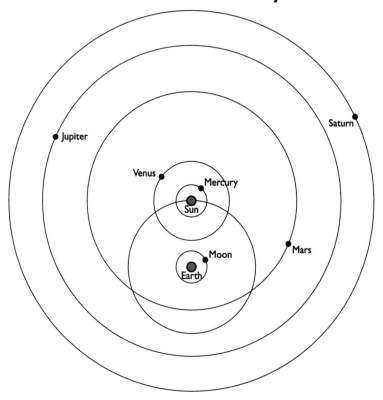

Kepler's Model of the Solar System

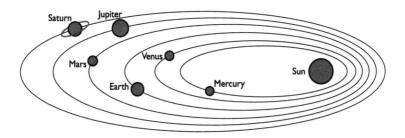

Compare Brahe's model of the universe to Kepler's. Even though both men see the same thing, the way in which they perceive what is happening is totally different.

Cognitive Universals and Cognitive Architecture

There is evidence that there are certain cultural, linguistic, and cognitive universals among all people, regardless of their specific group, and the existence of these universals goes against descriptive relativism.

Arguments Against Normative Relativism
The Mediation Problem

The most basic premise of the mediation problem is the notion that concepts, beliefs, and epistemic standards become trapped. This trapping prevents individuals from seeing if the beliefs and concepts match reality. One of the most popular versions of the mediation problem states that one is not able to think without having concepts, or talk without words. Therefore, it is impossible to go beyond our concepts or words in order to assess how the world truly is.

The Unintelligibility That Results from Extrapolation

Relativism often involves drawing conclusions about one group that is different from another group. However, just because one can coherently imagine concepts and beliefs that differ in some small way, does not mean that one can imagine concepts and beliefs that differ in great ways. In fact, when one attempts to extrapolate from such differences, it might lead to incoherence and unintelligibility.

Transcendental Arguments

The most famous transcendental arguments were made by Immanuel Kant, who claimed that concepts (which he called "categories") such as objects, property, causation, etc., must first exist in order for a person to experience things in space and time, and that humans are justified to use such concepts and have such beliefs.

EASTERN PHILOSOPHY

Philosophies from the other side of the world

Eastern philosophy refers to the philosophies that came about from the various regions of Asia (to a certain extent, the philosophies that came out of the Middle East have also been grouped into this term). The notion of Eastern philosophy can be a misleading one, however, due in part to the wide variety of cultures it encompasses. The philosophies that came out of China, for example, are drastically different than those that came from India.

In a very general sense, however, if the goals of Western philosophy are defined as seeking out and proving the notion of "truth," then the goals of Eastern philosophy are defined as accepting "truths" and finding balance. While Western philosophy places emphasis on the individual and the rights of the individual, Eastern philosophy emphasizes unity, social responsibility, and the interrelation of everything (which, in turn, cannot be separated from the cosmic whole). It is for this reason that, oftentimes, schools of Eastern philosophy are indistinguishable from the different religions of the land.

INDIAN PHILOSOPHY

The various philosophies to come out of India, called *darshanas* in Sanskrit, are disciplines that set out to improve life. These include orthodox schools (Hindu philosophies) and heterodox schools (non-Hindu philosophies).

Orthodox Schools

The orthodox, or Hindu, schools draw philosophical principles from the ancient Hindu sacred text, the Vedas.

Samkhya

The oldest of the orthodox philosophical schools is Samkhya. This philosophical system states that all things in reality come from *prakriti* (meaning energy, matter, and creative agency) and *purusha* (meaning the soul, mind, or self). Samkhya is based on dualism; however, unlike Western philosophy's definition of dualism as being between the mind and body, the dualism of Samkhya is based on the soul (an eternal, indivisible, and absolute reality that is pure consciousness) and matter. Total liberation occurs when one understands the differences between the soul and dispositions of matter (such as dullness, activity, and steadiness).

Yoga

The Yoga school draws upon the metaphysics and psychology of Samkhya; however, it features the presence of a divine entity. The goal of Yoga, as laid out in the Yoga Sutras (written in the second century B.C.), is to quiet the mind in order to attain a solitariness or detachment known as *kaivalya*.

Nyaya

The Nyaya philosophical school greatly influenced many other Indian schools of thought. The Nyaya philosophy is based on a system of logic, and followers believe that obtaining knowledge that is valid comes from inference, perception, testimony, and comparison. By obtaining knowledge in these ways, one becomes released from suffering. The Nyaya school also created criteria to determine what knowledge is valid and what knowledge is invalid.

Vaisheshika

Created in the sixth century B.C., the Vaisheshika school is based on pluralism and atomism. According to Vaisheshika, everything in the physical universe can be reduced to a finite number of atoms, and Brahman (the ultimate reality behind the gods and the universe) is what creates consciousness in the atoms. Eventually, the Nyaya and Vaisheshika schools merged together; however, Vaisheshika only accepted the sources of valid knowledge to be inference and perception.

Purva Mimamsa

The Purva Mimamsa school was based on interpreting the Vedas and being the authority on the sacred text. Purva Mimamsa involved an absolute faith in the sacred text and included the performance of fire-sacrifices in order to, it was believed, sustain the universe. While the Purva Mimamsa school believed in the philosophical and logical teachings of other schools, they argued that the only way one could attain salvation was by living in accordance with the teachings of the Vedas. Later on, the Purva Mimamsa school shifted to insist that in order to release one's soul, one must partake in enlightened activity.

Vedanta

The Vedanta school focused on the philosophical teachings of the mystic contemplations that were found within the Vedas, known as the Upanishads. The Vedanta school emphasized the importance of meditation, spiritual connectivity, and self-discipline.

Heterodox Schools

The four heterodox, or non-Hindu, schools did not accept the authority that was present in the Vedas.

Carvaka

This school was based on materialism, atheism, and skepticism. Perception, according to the Carvaka school, is the only valid source of knowledge.

Indian Political Philosophy

Political philosophy in India dates back to the fourth century B.C., with the *Arthashastra*, a text that discusses economic policy and statecraft. In the twentieth century, another political philosophy was made popular by Mahatma Gandhi and was greatly influenced by the writings of Jesus, Leo Tolstoy, John Ruskin, Henry David Thoreau, and the Hindu Bhagavad Gita. Gandhi emphasized a political philosophy based on *ahimsa*, or nonviolence, and satyagraha, or nonviolent resistance.

Buddhism

The philosophical principles of Buddhism are based on the Four Noble Truths (the truth of suffering, the truth of the cause of suffering, the truth of the end of suffering, and the truth of the path that frees one from suffering). Buddhism advocates that in order to end suffering, one must follow the Noble Eightfold Path. The philosophy of Buddhism touches on ethics, metaphysics, epistemology, phenomenology, and the notion that God is irrelevant.

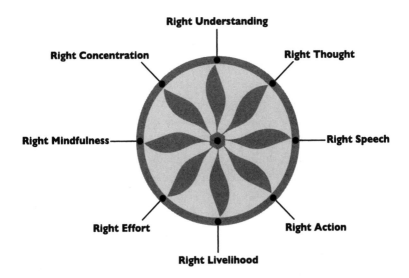

Right Understanding
Right Thought
Right Speech
Right Action
Right Livelihood
Right Effort
Right Mindfulness
Right Concentration

Jainism

One of the most basic ideas in Jainism is *anekantavada*, the notion that different points of view perceive reality differently, and therefore, there are no points of view that are completely true. In Jain philosophy, the only people who have true knowledge and know the true answer are referred to as Kevalis; anyone else can only know part of an answer. Jainism places great emphasis on equality of life, spiritual independence, nonviolence, and the fact that an individual's behavior has immediate consequences. Self-control, according to Jain philosophy, is crucial for one to understand the soul's true nature.

CHINESE PHILOSOPHY

The four most influential philosophical schools to come out of Chinese philosophy came about in 500 B.C. (the same time that ancient Greek philosophy began to emerge), and this period is referred to as the "Contention of a Hundred Schools of Thought." The dominant philosophical schools were Confucianism, Taoism, Mohism, and Legalism. During the various Chinese dynasties, these schools of thought, along with Buddhism, became incorporated into official doctrine.

Confucianism

Based on the teachings of Confucius, Confucianism was a philosophical system that touched on subjects related to politics, society, and morality, and was quasireligious in nature (though it was not a religion and allowed for one to follow a faith while still following Confucianism). Confucius created the idea of a meritocracy, the Golden Rule (which states that one should treat others as they would wish to be treated), the notion of yin and yang (two forces that oppose one another are permanently in conflict, which, in turn, creates endless change and contradiction), and the idea that in order to find middle ground, one must reconcile opposites. The major ideas of Confucianism are *ren* (humanness for others), *zhengming* (a rectification of names), *zhong* (loyalty), *xiao* (filial piety, a respect for one's parents and elders), and *li* (ritual).

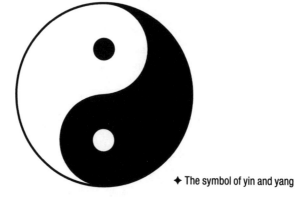

✦ The symbol of yin and yang

Taoism

Taoism began as a philosophy and later turned into a religion. *Tao* means "way" or "path," and is often used in a metaphysical way to represent the flow of the universe or the drive behind the natural order. Taoist philosophy focuses on humanism, relativism, emptiness, spontaneity, flexibility, and nonaction. Like Confucianism, Taoism places great emphasis on yin and yang, and it also places great importance on the Eight Trigrams, eight interrelated principles of reality, and feng shui, an ancient Chinese system of laws that uses colors and arrangement to attain harmony and balance in flow of energy.

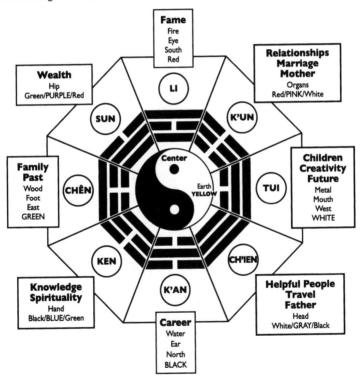

Legalism

Legalism was a political philosophy based on the idea that there should be strict and clear laws for people to abide by, or else there will be harsh punishment. Legalism is based on jurisprudence, meaning "philosophy of law." Legalism states that rulers should govern based on *Fa* (law), *Shu* (tactic, art, method, and managing state affairs), and *Shi* (power, charisma, or legitimacy).

Mohism

Mohism seeks mutual benefit by supporting the idea of universal love. According to Mohism, in order to avoid war and conflict, everybody must love one another equally. The founder of Mohism, Mozi (470–390 B.C.), was against the ritualistic teachings of Confucius, and instead believed that people should involve themselves in more practical ways to survive, such as farming, fortification, and managing state affairs.

Buddhism

As Buddhism spread to China, other schools of thought like Taoism and Confucianism were integrated into it, creating new Buddhist schools. These new types of Buddhism focused more on ethics and less on metaphysics.

KOREAN PHILOSOPHY

The philosophical schools to come out of Korea were greatly influenced by other philosophical schools of the area. The most significant philosophical schools were Shamanism, Confucianism, Taoism, and Buddhism.

Native Shamanism

Though later Shamanism would become influenced by Taoist and Buddhist thought, native Shamanism had developed in Korea for thousands of years. Shamanism is the belief that there exist helpful and harmful spirits within the natural world, and that only people with special powers, shamans, can address these spirits. A shaman in Korea was usually a woman, and was referred to as a *mudang*. The *mudang* would connect with the spirit world and attempt to fix human problems.

Buddhism

When Buddhism was brought to Korea from China in the year 372 A.D., Shaman spirits were incorporated into the philosophical school of thought in an effort to resolve what Koreans viewed as internal inconsistencies with the Chinese form of Buddhism.

Confucianism

Confucianism was also brought over to Korea from China. In fact, Confucianism had quite a significant impact on Korean society, molding its system of morality and legal system, and shaping the relations between the young and old. The most important ideas that were encouraged by Korean Confucian schools (also known as Neo-Confucianism) were *hyo* (filial piety), *chung* (loyalty), *sin* (trust), and *in* (benevolence).

Taoism

Taoism arrived in Korea from China in 674 A.D. While Korean Taoism was popular during the beginning of the Goryeo Dynasty (918–1392), by the middle period, Taoism, along with other philosophies and religions, became incorporated into Buddhism. Taoism never became its own religion in Korea, but its influence can still be found in Korean thought.

Korean Philosophy of the Modern Era

In 1910, due to Japanese rule, Shintoism became the official state religion of Korea. Also during this time, however, German idealist philosophers became very popular. When Korea was divided into North Korea and South Korea, North Korea began to follow orthodox Marxism, also incorporating ideas from Chinese Maoism and the notion of the *yangban* (ruling class) from Korean Confucianism.

JAPANESE PHILOSOPHY

Japanese philosophy is a fusion of Japanese, Chinese, and Western philosophies. While Taoism and Confucianism were present and influential in Japan, the presence of Shintoism and Buddhism were most impactful.

Shinto

The native religion of Japan, and its state religion until World War II, is known as Shinto. While Shinto itself is not necessarily a philosophy, it had a profound impact on the philosophies that emerged from Japan. Shintoism is a form of polytheistic animism in which the world is explained through powers and invisible spirits known as *kami*. When Buddhism was introduced to Japan in the sixth century from China and Korea, many elements of Buddhism were incorporated into Shintoism. Though there are no binding dogmatic principles within Shinto, importance is placed on key ideas like having a deep love and respect for nature, tradition and family, cleanliness, and festivals, known as *matsuri*, that celebrate the *kami*.

Buddhism

Buddhism was brought to Japan in 550 A.D. There are three main schools of Buddhism from Japan, and with the introduction of each new school, new philosophical ideas were introduced.

Zen Buddhism

Zen Buddhism was brought to Japan from Korea (which got it from China, whose version was based on the Indian Mahayana Buddhist teachings) and became its own school of thought in the twelfth century. The principles of Zen Buddhism claim that every sentient being has an inherent virtue and wisdom (Buddha-nature) hidden within his mind. According to Zen Buddhism, through meditation and being mindful of one's day-to-day experiences, one is able to uncover his Buddha-nature. Currently, there exist three schools of Zen Buddhism in Japan:

1. Soto (the largest of the schools)
2. Rinzai (which has many schools within it)
3. Obaku (the smallest of the schools)

Amidist Buddhism

Amidist, also known as Pure Land, Buddhism is one of the more popular forms of Buddhism in Japan and China, and is based on the teachings of the Amitabha Buddha. According to this type of Buddhism, enlightenment is guaranteed if one devotes his life to having a relationship with Amitabha Buddha (the most basic practice to do so is chanting the name of Amitabha Buddha with complete concentration), and a person who is enlightened will be reborn in the Pure Land.

Nichiren Buddhism

Nichiren Buddhism is based on the philosophical teachings of the Japanese monk Nichiren, who lived during the thirteenth century. One of the main beliefs of Nichiren Buddhism is that since people have an innate Buddha-nature within themselves, they are able to attain enlightenment in this lifetime and in their current form.

Influence of Western Philosophy

The philosophical movement known as the Kyoto School emerged during the twentieth century. The movement was based at Kyoto University and incorporated many ideas of Western philosophy and religion into traditional East Asian ideas. Specifically, the ideas of Hegel, Kant, Heidegger, Nietzsche, and Christianity were used to reformulate moral and religious understanding.

AVICENNA (980–1037)

The most influential philosopher of the Islamic Golden Age

Ibn Sina (also referred to by the Latinized name Avicenna) lived from 980 to 1037 in what is now Uzbekistan. Avicenna was a Persian philosopher and physician, and is considered to be the most important figure of the Islamic Golden Age.

Avicenna was an exceptional physician and wrote medical books that would have an incredible impact on not only the Islamic world, but medical schools and thought across Europe. In addition to his medical writings, however, he also wrote extensively on metaphysics, ethics, and logic, and his philosophies regarding the soul and the essence of existence were incredibly influential in Western philosophy.

AVICENNA AND THE ISLAMIC GOLDEN AGE

The Islamic Golden Age occurred during the Middle Ages, when Europe was deeply involved in religious dogmatism and made relatively little headway in terms of philosophy. While philosophy in Europe was stagnant, philosophy in the Islamic world flourished, largely due to the work of Avicenna. Avicenna is considered to be one of the most important figures of this era, and he was one of the main people to introduce the works of Aristotle, as well as Neoplatonic ideas, to the Islamic world.

AVICENNA'S METAPHYSICS: ESSENCE AND EXISTENCE

Avicenna argued that essence (known as *Mahiat*) is independent from existence (known as *Wujud*), and is eternal and unchanging. He claimed that essence came before existence, and that existence is simply accidental. Therefore, according to Avicenna, anything that comes into existence is the result of an essence allowing for that existence.

His notion of essence and existence is similar to Plato's theory of Forms (the idea that everything that exists falls under a pre-existing archetype and that even when something no longer exists, the archetype remains); however, Avicenna claimed that Allah (the First Reality) is the only thing in the world that was not preceded by an essence. Allah, according to Avicenna, is a necessary being that one cannot define. If one attempts to define Allah, the very act of defining creates opposition. For example, if one were to say, "Allah is beautiful," that must then also mean that "Allah is not ugly," but this cannot be the case because everything comes from Allah.

Logic

Avicenna, a devout Muslim, believed that logic and reason could be used to prove the existence of God, and often, he used logic to interpret the Qur'an. Avicenna claimed that logic can be used to judge those concepts that are acquired via the four faculties of reason: estimation (*wahm*), retention (*al-khayal*), sense-perception (*al-hiss al-mushtarak*), and imagination (*al-mutakhayyila*). Imagination, according to Avicenna, is crucial because it allows for an individual to be able to compare new phenomena to concepts that already exist.

Avicenna also believed logic could be used to acquire new knowledge, make deductions, help an individual judge whether or not an argument is valid, and share knowledge with others. In order for one to attain salvation, Avicenna believed one has to gain knowledge and perfect his intellect.

EPISTEMOLOGY AND THE TEN INTELLECTS

Avicenna's own theory of creation stems largely from the theory of Al-Farabi, another famous Islamic philosopher. According to this theory, the creation of the world followed the First Intellect. The First Intellect begins to contemplate its own existence, and in doing so, the Second Intellect is created. As the Second Intellect begins to contemplate its origins from God, the First Spirit is created, which then sparks the universe, known as the Sphere of Spheres. As the Sphere of Spheres contemplates that it is something that has the potential to exist, it creates matter. This matter fills the universe and creates the Sphere of the Planets.

It is from the triple-contemplation that the early stages of existence emerge. As the process continues, two celestial hierarchies are created as a result of the continuation of emerging intellects: the Inferior Hierarchy (which Avicenna refers to as the "Angels of Magnificence") and the Superior Hierarchy of Cherubim. According to Avicenna, the angels, which are responsible for prophetic visions in humans, are deprived of sensory perception. They do, however, have imagination, and this imagination lets them desire the intellect that they originated from. The angels' journey to rejoin with their respective intellect creates eternal movement in heaven.

The following seven intellects, and the angels created by them, correspond to different bodies within the Sphere of Planets. They are Jupiter, Mars, Saturn, Venus, Mercury, the sun, and the moon (which is associated with the Angel Gabriel, "The Angel"). It is from the ninth intellect that humans emerge (featuring the sensory functions that the angels lack).

Avicenna then claims that the tenth and final intellect is human intellect. He claims that on its own, the human mind is not formed for abstract thought. Avicenna claims that in humans, there is only the potential for intellect, and that this potential can only come about through illumination by The Angel. This illumination can vary in degrees; prophets, for example, have been illuminated so much that they can have rational intellect, imagination, and the ability to pass their information on to others, while other people might have only enough illumination to teach, write, pass down information, and pass laws, and others might receive even less illumination. Here we see Avicenna's view of humanity as having a collective consciousness.

AVICENNA'S FLOATING MAN

To demonstrate the self-awareness and immateriality of the soul, Avicenna created his famous thought experiment known as the "Floating Man." In the Floating Man thought experiment, Avicenna asks the reader to imagine a scenario in which he is suspended in the air. As the individual hangs in the air, he will experience complete isolation from his senses (which means that he will not even have sensory contact with his own body).

Avicenna argued that even with this isolation from the senses, a person would still have self-consciousness. If a person that is isolated from sense experience still has the ability to determine his own existence, according to Avicenna, this shows that the soul is an immaterial substance that exists independent of the body. Avicenna also claimed that since this scenario is conceivable, it points to the conclusion that the soul is perceived intellectually.

Furthermore, Avicenna believed that the brain is where reason and sensation interact with one another. In the scenario of the Floating Man, the very first knowledge that the individual would have is "I am," which affirms that individual's essence. Because the individual is isolated from sense experience, essence cannot come from the body. Therefore, the very core of a person is the knowledge "I am," which means not only does the soul exist; the soul is self-aware. Avicenna concluded that not only is the soul an immaterial substance; it is perfect.

BERTRAND RUSSELL (1872–1970)

The logistic philosopher

Bertrand Russell was born on May 18, 1872, in Ravenscroft, Wales. By the time Russell was just four years old, he had lost both his mother and father, and he and his older brother lived with their very strict grandparents (his grandfather, Lord John Russell, was a former Prime Minister and the first Earl of Russell). When Russell was six years old, his grandfather had died too, leaving him and his brother with only their grandmother. At a young age, Russell wished to free himself from the household filled with prohibitions and rules, and this desire, as well as a distrust of religion, would have a profound impact on the rest of his life.

In 1890, Russell attended Trinity College, Cambridge, where he excelled in mathematics and philosophy. Russell initially became quite interested in idealism (the idea that reality is a product of the mind), though years after leaving Cambridge, he would reject idealism entirely, in favor of realism (the idea that consciousness and experience exist independently from the external world) and empiricism (the idea that knowledge comes from sensory experiences from the external world).

The early work of Bertrand Russell focused on mathematics. Russell's defense of logicism (the notion that all mathematics can be reduced to appear as logical principles) was incredibly important, and if it were proven true, it would show that mathematics is legitimately *a priori* knowledge. While his philosophical ideas touched many subjects throughout the span of his life (including morality, the philosophy of language, metaphysics, and linguistics), Russell always continued working in logic, and wrote a three-volume book, *Principia Mathematica*, to show that all mathematical principles, arithmetic, and numbers stem from logic.

Russell, along with his student, Ludwig Wittgenstein, and philosopher G. E. Moore, are considered to be the founders of analytic philosophy.

Philosophical Definitions

ANALYTIC PHILOSOPHY: Considered to be both a historical tradition and a method of practice, analytic philosophy (which has also become synonymous with logical positivism) is the idea that one should practice and execute philosophy in the same way that one would practice and execute scientific inquiry: with precision and rigor. This is done through the use of logic and being skeptical of assumptions.

Though he was a philosopher, mathematician, and logician, Bertrand Russell first became familiar to people as a result of his controversial beliefs about social reform. Russell was an active pacifist during World War I and attended several protests, which not only got him dismissed from Trinity College, but ultimately landed him in jail. Later, during World War II, while tirelessly campaigning against Adolf Hitler and the Nazi Party, he rejected his pacifist ideas for more of a relativist approach. Russell also became an outspoken critic of Stalin's totalitarian regime, of the United States's involvement in the Vietnam War, and of nuclear disarmament. Bertrand Russell was awarded the Nobel Prize in Literature in 1950.

LOGICAL ATOMISM

Bertrand Russell created logical atomism, the idea that one can break down language into its smallest parts, much like physical matter. Once a sentence has been broken down so much so that those small parts can no longer be broken down, those parts are considered to be "logical atoms." If we then look at these logical atoms, we should be able to uncover underlying assumptions of a sentence and then be able to better determine whether it is valid or true.

For example, let's take a look at the following sentence: "The king of the United States is bald."

This sentence seems simple; however, from it, we can break it down into three logical atoms.

1. The king of the United States exists.
2. There is one king of the United States.
3. The king of the United States does not have hair.

Since we know that there is no king of the United States, the first atom proves to be false. Therefore, the sentence "The king of the United States is bald" is untrue. However, this does not necessarily mean it is properly false, because the opposite of this statement, "The king of the United States has hair," is also untrue. In both cases, it is assumed that the United States has a king. Through logical atomism, we are able to see the validity and degree of truth. This raises the question that is still being debated to this day: If something is not true or false, then what is it?

THEORY OF DESCRIPTIONS

Bertrand Russell's most important contribution to linguistics is his theory of descriptions. According to Russell, truth cannot be represented by common language because it is too ambiguous and misleading. Russell claimed that in order for philosophy to be free of assumptions and mistakes, a different, more thorough, type of language is required. Russell then claimed that this language should be based on mathematical logic and appear more like a series of mathematical equations.

In trying to answer the questions brought on by the sentence "The king of the United States is bald," Russell created his theory of descriptions. For Russell, definite descriptions are names, phrases, or words that pertain to a single, specific object (like "that table," "Australia," or "Steven Spielberg"). If a sentence contains definite descriptions, according to Russell, it is actually a shorthand way to express a group of claims within a series. Therefore, Russell was able to show that grammar obscures the logical form of a sentence. However, in "The king of the United States is bald," the object that is being described is nonexistent or ambiguous (which Russell refers to as "incomplete symbols").

SET THEORY AND RUSSELL'S PARADOX

As Bertrand Russell attempted to reduce all types of mathematics into logic, the notion of a "set" became very important. Russell defines a set as "a collection of members or elements" (in other words, objects). Sets can be defined negatively or feature subsets, which can then be added or subtracted. For example, a set might be all Americans; a set defined negatively might be all things that are not Americans; and a subset within a set might be all New Yorkers within the set of all Americans.

While Bertrand Russell was not the first person to create set theory (that was Gottlob Frege), Russell completely revolutionized the founding principles of the theory with his introduction of "Russell's paradox" in 1901.

Russell's paradox deals with the set of every set that is not a member of itself. For example, let's look at a set of all of the dogs that ever existed. The set of every dog that ever existed is not also a dog, but there do exist some sets that are members of themselves. If we look at the set that is made up of everything that is not a dog, for example, this must mean that even the set has to be included because that set is also not a dog.

When one tries to think of a set that is made up of sets that aren't members of themselves, the result is a paradox. Why? Because we see a set containing sets that are not members of themselves, and yet by the very definition of the original set (a set that is made up of sets that aren't members of themselves), this means that it must also include itself. However, its very definition states that it cannot include itself, and therefore a contradiction appears.

It is from Russell's paradox that we see the imperfections of set theory. By calling any group of objects a set, situations that are logically impossible can appear. Russell claims that in order to fix this flaw, set theory has to be stricter. Sets, according to Russell, can only pertain to particular collections that satisfy specific axioms (thus avoiding the impossibility and contradiction that can appear from the current model). It is because of the work of Bertrand Russell that all set theory work prior to Russell is known as naïve set theory, and all set theory work after Russell is known as axiomatic set theory.

PHENOMENOLOGY

The study of consciousness

Phenomenology is the study of consciousness and personal experience. Phenomenology started to become a major branch of philosophical study during the twentieth century, particularly showcased by the works of Heidegger and Sartre. However, neither Heidegger nor Sartre would have been able to achieve as much as they did if it were not for the work of Edmund Husserl, the founder of phenomenology.

THE ORIGIN OF PHENOMENOLOGY

Moravian philosopher Edmund Husserl began his career as a mathematician and focused on the philosophy of mathematics. While he originally believed arithmetic followed strict empiricism, through the help of Gottlob Frege, Husserl concluded that certain arithmetic truths cannot be explained through empiricism. In his book, *The Logical Investigations*, Husserl argued against "psychologism," the idea that truths are dependent of the psychology (mind) of an individual, and asserted that truths cannot be reduced by the human mind. From this idea, Husserl began to develop phenomenology.

Phenomenology, according to Husserl, is the idea that consciousness has intentionality. This means that all acts of consciousness are directed at objects, be they material or ideal (such as mathematics). Intentional objects of consciousness and intentional acts of consciousness are both defined through consciousness. In order for one to describe the object of consciousness and content of consciousness, it is also not necessary for the object to actually exist (allowing for someone to describe what happened in a dream in the same way he could describe a scene in a book).

While Husserl's early work was based on a realist approach (believing that when one's consciousness perceives an object, it means there are both objects of consciousness and the objects themselves), Husserl's later work shifted more toward intentionality and the study of ego. Husserl's evolving stance and turn toward transcendental ideas would come to reinvent the very subject he started.

In Husserl's 1931 book, *Ideas: A General Introduction to Pure Phenomenology*, he makes a distinction between a person's natural standpoint, which is the ordinary viewpoint where an individual is only aware of those things factually present, and a person's phenomenological standpoint, where an individual sees past the external object and comes to understand the consciousness of the object. In order to attain a phenomenological standpoint, one must eliminate various features of his experience by undergoing a series of phenomenological reductions.

Husserl created many phenomenological reductions; however, two of the most noteworthy phenomenological reductions include epoché and the reduction proper.

Epoché

Husserl claimed that people take the various aspects of their lives (language, culture, gravity, their bodies, etc.) for granted, and that these aspects are keeping people in captivity. The epoché, however, is the phenomenological reduction where one no longer accepts these aspects to be true. An individual must attain a self-consciousness by seeing himself as no longer a part of the things that he has come to accept in the world. Husserl refers to this process as "bracketing."

Bracketing does not mean denying the world's existence—the entire purpose of bracketing and the epoché is to abstain from all belief, and therefore one can neither confirm nor deny the world's existence.

The Reduction Proper

While the epoché describes the method one uses to no longer accept the accepted and to become free from the captivity of the accepted world, the reduction proper is the process of recognizing the acceptance as just that: an acceptance. It is by being able to see an acceptance as an acceptance that one can attain a transcendental insight.

Together, the reduction proper and epoché make up the process of phenomenological reduction. Note that the reduction proper cannot act independently from the epoché, and vice versa.

THE METHOD OF PHENOMENOLOGICAL INVESTIGATION

According to Husserl, the first step of phenomenological investigation is phenomenological reduction (through epoché and the reduction proper). This bracketing of everything one is aware of includes all modes of consciousness (like imagination, recollection, judgment, and intuition).

The next step is known as eidetic reduction. It is simply not enough to have consciousness. Rather, one has to make the various acts of consciousness obtainable to a point that their very essences, the structures that cannot be changed and are universal, can be attained. A type of intuition that one can use to do this is known as

"*Wesensschau*." In *Wesensschau*, one has to create multiple variations and focus in on what part of the multiplicity remains unchanged. This is the essence, for it is the one identical part throughout all of the variations.

The third and final step is known as transcendental reduction. For Husserl, phenomenology meant returning one to his transcendental ego (the self that is required for there to be a complete, united, and empirical self-consciousness) as the foundation for creating meaning. Husserl claimed that in order to reach the transcendental ego, there must be a reversal of the transcendental consciousness, and that within this consciousness is the creation of time awareness that acts as a self-constitution.

While Husserl would spend the rest of his career attempting to clarify transcendental reduction, the very idea of transcendental reduction sparked controversy. As a result, a division occurred within phenomenology between those who believed in transcendental reduction and those who refused to believe in transcendental reduction.

PHENOMENOLOGY OF ESSENCES

When students of Theodor Lipps (the creator of psychologism) in Munich decided to follow the philosophical work of Husserl instead, they left Munich and joined with Husserl's students in Göttingen. However, when, in 1913, Husserl published his thoughts on transcendental reduction in his book *Ideas*, they completely disagreed with Husserl's theories and distanced themselves from his new work. In doing so, they created a new type of phenomenology, known as phenomenology of essences, which was based on the realist phenomenology of Husserl's earlier work.

NOMINALISM

Rejecting certain elements

In philosophy, nominalism has two meanings. The more traditional definition of nominalism, which came about during the Middle Ages, involves a rejection of universals, entities that can be represented by different objects. The second, more modern, use of the word pertains to a rejection of abstract objects, objects that are not temporal or spatial. Therefore, nominalism can be seen as the opposite of realism (the belief that universals do exist) and as the opposite of Platonism (the belief that abstract objects do exist). It is possible for one to believe in one type of nominalism and not the other.

Both types of nominalism deal with antirealism because they both deny the existence of universals or abstract objects, and therefore also deny the reality of these things. In dealing with things that are alleged to be abstract objects or universals, nominalism takes two approaches:

1. Nominalism denies that the alleged entities exist.
2. Nominalism accepts that the entities exist, but claims the entities are not concrete or particular.

ABSTRACT OBJECTS

There is no set definition of what an abstract object is; however, the common explanation is "an object that does not exist in space or time and is causally inert" (it is assumed that only objects that exist in space and time can partake in causal relations). This definition, however, is not without its flaws. For example, while language and games are abstract, they are both temporal (since languages can change, develop, and come into being at different times). While philosophers have provided other definitions of an abstract object, nominalism is driven by the rejection of spatiotemporal objects that are causally inert.

UNIVERSALS

Nominalists distinguish between universals and particulars. According to nominalism's definition, universals refer to anything that is instantiated (meaning represented through an actual thing) by multiple entities. If it is not, then it is a particular. Both a universal and a particular can instantiate an entity, but only a universal has the ability to be instantiated by multiple entities. For example, objects that are red cannot have an instance, but with the universal "redness," any object that is red is an instance of that universal. Realists consider properties (like redness), kinds (like the material, gold), and relations (like between-ness) to be examples of universals. Nominalism about universals rejects this notion.

TYPES OF NOMINALISM ABOUT UNIVERSALS

Those who follow nominalism about universals believe that only particulars exist. To explain the existence of relations or properties, two accepted strategies appear throughout philosophy: the first is to reject that these entities exist, and the second is to accept the existence of these entities while denying that the entities are universals.

Trope Theory

Of the latter form of arguments, one of the most popular theories is known as trope theory. In trope theory, one believes in the existence of properties (thereby accepting the existence of the entity) but believes that properties are specific entities known as "tropes." Philosophers consider these tropes to be particulars, much like an individual peach or banana is its own particular. Therefore, the yellowness of a banana is not considered to be a universal, but rather a specific, or particular, yellowness that pertains only to this banana. The banana possesses this yellowness, which makes it a trope, because the yellowness is not the result of a universal being instantiated.

Concept Nominalism and Predicate Nominalism

Two other types of nominalism about universals are concept nominalism (also known as conceptualism) and predicate nominalism. Concept nominalism states that yellowness does not exist and that an entity, such as a banana, is yellow simply because it is in line with the concept of "yellow." Similarly, in predicate nominalism, a banana is yellow as a result of the predicate that "yellow" is applying to it. Therefore, there is no "yellowness," only the application of the predicate yellow.

Mereological Nominalism and Class Nominalism

In another type of nominalism about universals, mereological nominalism, the property of being yellow is the total of all yellow entities. Therefore, an entity is yellow because it is a part of the aggregate of those things that are yellow. Similarly, class nominalism claims that properties are considered to be classes. Therefore, the class of every yellow thing and only yellow things is the property of being yellow.

Resemblance Nominalism

Resemblance nominalism claims that yellow things do not resemble each other because of the fact that they are yellow; rather, it is the fact that they resemble each other that makes them yellow. According to resemblance nominalism, a banana is considered yellow because it resembles other things that are yellow. Therefore, definite resemblance conditions must be satisfied by all members of a specific class.

TYPES OF NOMINALISM ABOUT ABSTRACT OBJECTS

Nominalism about abstract objects is broken into two types: nominalism about propositions and nominalism about possible worlds.

Nominalism about Propositions

Entities within nominalism about propositions can be broken into two categories: unstructured and structured. Unstructured propositions are sets of possible worlds. Within these worlds, functions have the value of True (arguing the proposition is true) and the value of False (arguing the proposition is false).

One theory of nominalism about propositions claims that the roles connected with propositions are in fact played by objects that are concrete. A theory pertaining to this idea is the notion that sentences take on the role of propositions. Philosopher Willard van Orman Quine claimed that "eternal sentences" (sentences with a constant truth-value throughout) make for better truth-bearers because they are independent of place, time, speaker, etc. This, however, leads to a problem for nominalists because the very idea of an eternal sentence is an abstract object.

Semantic Fictionalism

Another option in nominalism about propositions is to deny the existence of propositions and all entities that have theoretical roles. If this is the case, sentences that involve the existence of propositions that seem to be true must actually be false. Even if a sentence is false because there are no propositions, however, it can still be used as a descriptive aid. This descriptive aid allows one to clarify what he wants to say and allows for the representation of parts of the world's structure.

Nominalism about Possible Worlds

The possible worlds theory is a much-debated philosophical idea that accounts for other realities by claiming that this world is only one of many possible worlds that exist. A nominalist can assume that there are no possible worlds or that possible worlds are not abstract objects.

One nominalist approach is to believe that not every possible world exists, and that only actual possible worlds exist. One can think of actual possible worlds as being sums of spatiotemporal objects that are related to one another, which is actually the sum of concrete objects.

Another nominalist way to look at possible worlds is to view what is possible as a combination of elements (universals and particulars). According to this theory, a state of affairs that has a universal as a property consists of a particular and a universal coming together, and a state of affairs that consists of a universal as a relation is when a universal and some particulars come together. There is a wide range of possible combinations for particulars and universals, and the result is that some are actualized while others are not.

GOTTFRIED WILHELM LEIBNIZ (1646–1716)

The optimistic philosopher

Gottfried Wilhelm Leibniz was one of the most important philosophers of the seventeenth-century rationalist movement. In addition to his work in rationalism, Leibniz was quite versatile and made great strides in subjects like logic, physics, and mathematics (he invented calculus independently of Newton and discovered the binary system).

Leibniz was born on July 1, 1646, in Leipzig, Germany. Leibniz's father was a professor of moral philosophy at the University of Leipzig, and when Gottfried was just six years old, his father died and left his personal library to the young Leibniz. In his father's absence, Leibniz learned religion and morality from his mother.

Leibniz was an incredibly gifted child. By the time he was twelve years old, he had already taught himself Latin and started learning Greek, and when he was fourteen years old, he began attending the University of Leipzig and took classes in Aristotelian philosophy, law, logic, and scholastic philosophy. When he was twenty years old, he published his first book, *On the Art of Combinations*, in which he claimed that combinations of basic elements, such as sound, colors, letters, and numbers, are the source of all discovery and reasoning.

After graduating from another school with a law degree, instead of further pursuing academia, he worked in service for noblemen. He wore many hats in this position, including acting as a legal advisor and official historian, and he was required to travel extensively throughout Europe. On his many travels, Leibniz met with several of Europe's most important intellectuals while at the same time working on his own mathematical and metaphysical problems. The men that had a particular influence on him during these times were philosopher Baruch Spinoza and mathematician, astronomer, and physicist Christiaan Huygens.

All of Leibniz's work, from his numerous contributions to mathematics to his vast and rich philosophical work, shares a common theme of emphasizing the truth. He hoped that, by emphasizing the truth through his work, he would be able to form a foundation capable of reuniting the divided church.

THE PRINCIPLES OF LEIBNIZ'S PHILOSOPHY

There are seven fundamental principles to Leibniz's understanding of reason:

1. **Identity/Contradiction:** If a proposition is true, its negation must be false, and vice versa.
2. **Sufficient Reason:** In order for anything to exist, any event to occur, or any truth to be had, there has to be a sufficient reason (though this is sometimes only known by God).
3. **Identity of Indiscernibles (Leibniz's Law):** Two things that are distinct from one another cannot have every single property in common. If all predicates possessed by X are also possessed by Y, and all predicates possessed by Y are also possessed by X, then X and Y are identical. To claim that two things are indiscernible is supposing two names for the same thing.

4. **Optimism:** God always chooses the best.
5. **Pre-Established Harmony:** Substances can only affect themselves; however, all substances (be they mind or body) causally interact with one another. This is the result of God having programmed all substances to harmonize with one another in advance.
6. **Plenitude:** The best of every possible world would make every genuine possibility a reality.
7. **Law of Continuity:** Leibniz states in his law of continuity that "nature never takes leaps." Leibniz claims that all change goes through intermediate change and that there is an infinity in things. The law of continuity is used to prove that no motion can come from total rest; perceptions come from other degrees of perception that are too small to notice.

THEORY OF MONADS

In rejecting Descartes's theory that matter, which has an essence of extension (meaning it exists in more than one dimension), is considered a substance, Leibniz created his theory of monads, which became one of his greatest contributions to metaphysics. Leibniz claimed that only those beings that are capable of action and have true unity can be considered a substance. According to Leibniz, monads are the elements that make up the universe. These are particles that are individual, eternal, un-interacting, affected by their own laws, and have a pre-established harmony in which the entire universe is reflected. These particles are the only true substances because they have unity and are capable of action.

Monads are not like atoms. They have no spatial character or material and are independent from one another. Monads "know" what to do at every moment because they are preprogrammed with individual instructions (via the law of pre-established harmony). Monads can also vary in size, unlike atoms. For example, every individual person can be viewed as an individual monad (which creates an argument against free will).

Leibniz's theory of monads gets rid of the dualism found in Descartes's work, and leads to Leibniz's theory of idealism. Monads are forms of being, meaning only they are considered mind-like entities and substance. As a result, things like matter, space, and motion are just phenomena that are the result of substances.

OPTIMISM

Leibniz attempted to bring religion and philosophy together in his 1710 book, *Théodicée*. Believing that God, who is all-powerful and all-knowing, would never create a world that is imperfect or choose to create a world that is imperfect when the possibility of having a better one exists, Leibniz concluded that this world must be the most balanced and best possible world there can be. Therefore, according to Leibniz, the flaws of this world have to exist in every possible world. Otherwise, those flaws would not have been included by God.

Leibniz believed that philosophy is not meant to contradict theology because reason and faith are gifts of God. Thus, if any part of faith cannot be supported by reason, it has to be rejected. With this in mind, Leibniz tackled a central criticism of Christianity: If God is all-powerful, all-wise, and all-good, how did evil come about? Leibniz states that God is all-powerful, all-wise, and all-good;

however, humans are God's creations, and as such, they have limited wisdom and power to act. Because humans are creations that have free will, they are predisposed to ineffective actions, wrong decisions, and false beliefs. God allows for pain and suffering (known as physical evil) and sin (known as moral evil) to exist because they are consequences that are necessary of imperfection (known as metaphysical evil) and so that humans can compare their imperfection to true good and correct their decisions.

ETHICS

Determining what is right and what is wrong

Ethics, also known as moral philosophy, involves understanding what makes one's conduct right and what makes it wrong. Ethics is much bigger than morality, however. While morality deals with moral codes and the practice of specific acts, ethics not only touches on all moral behaviors and theories, but also on one's philosophy of life. Ethics deals with questions such as how a person should act, what people think is right, how an individual uses and practices his moral knowledge, and the very meaning of "right."

NORMATIVE ETHICS

Normative ethics attempts to understand ethical action by creating a set of rules (or norms) that govern action and human conduct. Normative ethics looks at how things should be, how one should value things, what actions are right versus what actions are wrong, and which things are good versus which things are bad.

Following are three types of normative ethical theories.

Consequentialism

Morality of an action is based on the results or outcome of the action. If there is a good outcome, then an action is considered morally right; if there is a bad outcome, then an action is considered morally wrong. In consequentialism, philosophers examine what makes a consequence a good consequence, how one can judge a consequence and who should do the judging, and who gains the most from a moral action. Examples of consequentialism include hedonism, utilitarianism, and egoism.

Deontology

Instead of looking at the consequences of actions, deontology looks at how the actions themselves can be right and wrong. Those who believe in deontology claim that one should take into consideration factors such as the rights of others and one's own duty when making decisions. Types of deontology include the natural rights theories of John Locke and Thomas Hobbes, which claim that humans have universal and natural rights; the divine command theory, which states that God commands morally right actions and that an action is morally right when it is performed as a duty or obligation; and Immanuel Kant's categorical imperative, which argued that one must act based on duty, and that rightness and wrongness are based on the motives of the individual and not the consequences. According to Kant's categorical imperative, a person should think of his actions (and therefore act) as if the motivating principle of that action should be considered a universal law.

Virtue Ethics

In virtue ethics, philosophers look at the inherent character of an individual. Virtue ethics seeks out virtues, which are the behaviors and habits that allow one to have a good life or reach a state of well-being. It also provides counsel to fix conflicts between virtues and claims that in order to have a good life, one must practice these virtues for his entire life. Examples of virtue ethics include *eudaimonia*, which was created by Aristotle and states that an action is considered "right" when it leads to well-being and can be attained through the daily practice of virtues; agent-based theories, which claim that virtue is based on common-sense intuitions regarding admirable traits and that these can be identified by examining those people whom we admire; and ethics of care, which claims morality and virtues should be based on virtues that are exemplified by women (such as the ability to nurture, have patience, and take care of others).

META-ETHICS

Meta-ethics examines ethical judgments and specifically tries to understand statements, attitudes, judgments, and ethical properties. Meta-ethics is not concerned with evaluating whether or not a specific choice is good or bad. Rather, it examines the nature and meaning of the issue. There are two types of meta-ethical views: moral realism and moral antirealism.

Moral Realism

Moral realism is the belief that there are objective moral values. Therefore, according to this meta-ethical viewpoint, evaluative statements are actually factual claims, and whether these claims are true or false is independent from one's beliefs and feelings. This is known as a cognitivist view, where propositions that are valid are conveyed as ethical sentences, which can either be true or false. Examples of moral realism include:

- Ethical naturalism, the belief that we have empirical knowledge of objective moral properties (however, these can then be reduced to non-ethical properties, and therefore ethical properties can be reduced to natural properties).

- Ethical non-naturalism, the belief that ethical statements represent propositions that are impossible to deduce into nonethical statements.

Moral Antirealism

According to moral antirealism, there are no such things as objective moral values. There are three types of moral antirealism:

1. Ethical subjectivism (based on the notion that ethical statements are actually subjective claims)
2. Noncognitivism (the notion that ethical statements are not genuine claims)
3. The idea that ethical statements are mistaken objective claims (which is expressed through moral skepticism, the belief that nobody can have moral knowledge, or moral nihilism, the belief that ethical statements are usually false).

DESCRIPTIVE ETHICS

Descriptive ethics is free of any values and looks at ethics through the observations of actual choices made. Descriptive ethics looks at the beliefs people have with regard to morality, and there exists an implication that theories of conduct or value are real. The purpose of descriptive ethics is not to examine how reasonable a moral norm is, or to provide any sort of guidance. Rather, descriptive ethics compares ethical systems (like those of different societies, the past and present, etc.) and compares one's rules of conduct that explain an actual action with the ethics that one says he believes in. It is for this reason that descriptive ethics is frequently used by anthropologists, historians, and psychologists.

APPLIED ETHICS

Applied ethics attempts to bring ethical theory into real-life situations and is often used in creating public policy. Generally speaking, in applied ethics, approaches that are very strict and based on principles can solve particular problems, cannot be applied universally, and can sometimes be impossible to put into effect. Applied ethics can be used to explore such questions as what human rights are, whether abortions are immoral, what rights animals have, etc. There are many different types of applied ethics, including medical ethics (how moral judgments and values apply to medicine), legal ethics (ethics related to those who practice law), and media ethics (the ethical issues that pertain to entertainment, journalism, and marketing).

PHILOSOPHY OF SCIENCE

What is science?

In discussing the philosophy of science, philosophers generally focus on natural sciences like biology, chemistry, astronomy, physics, and earth science, and examine the implications, assumptions, and foundations that result from this science. Generally speaking, the criteria for science are:

1. The creation of hypotheses. These hypotheses must meet the logical criteria of contingency (meaning logically speaking, they are not necessarily true or false), falsifiability (meaning they have the ability to be proven false), and testability (meaning there are real chances that the hypotheses could be established as true or as false).
2. A grounding in empirical evidence.
3. Use of the scientific method.

THE DEMARCATION PROBLEM

According to philosopher Karl Popper, the central question in the philosophy of science is known as the demarcation problem. Put simply, the demarcation problem is how one can distinguish between science and non-science (this question also deals with pseudoscience in particular). To this day, there is still not a generally accepted account of the demarcation problem, and some even find it to be insignificant or find it unsolvable. While logical positivists, who combined empiricism with logic, tried to ground science in observation and claimed that anything that is nonobservational is non-science (and meaningless), Popper claimed that the main property of science is falsifiability.

Philosophical Definitions

FALSIFIABILITY: In order for a hypothesis to be accepted as true, and before any hypothesis can be accepted as a scientific theory or scientific hypothesis, it has to be disprovable.

In other words, for Popper, any scientific claim could be proven to be false. If, after extensive effort, no such proof can be found, then it must mean that the claim is most likely true.

THE VALIDITY OF SCIENTIFIC REASONING

Scientific reasoning can be grounded in many different ways to show that theories are valid.

Induction

It can be difficult for a scientist to state that a law is universally true because even if every test brings back the same results, that doesn't necessarily mean that future tests will also have the same results. It is for this reason that scientists use induction. According to inductive reasoning, if a situation holds true in every observed case, then it holds true in all cases.

Empirical Verification

Scientific claims need evidence in order to back up theories or models. Therefore, the predictions that scientific theories and models can make must be in agreement with the evidence that has already been observed (and observations are ultimately results coming from the senses). Observations have to be agreed upon by others and be repeatable, and predictions must be specific so that a scientist can falsify a theory or model (which implies the prediction) with an observation.

The Duhem-Quine Thesis and Occam's Razor

The Duhem-Quine thesis states that it is not possible to test a theory or hypothesis in complete isolation because in order for one to empirically test a hypothesis, one must involve other background assumptions. A result of this thesis is the notion that any theory can have the ability to be compatible with empirical information if enough ad hoc hypotheses are included. It is for this reason that Occam's razor (the notion that the simplest of explanations should be chosen among competing theories) is used in science. In agreeing with the Duhem-Quine thesis, Karl Popper shifted from favoring a naive falsification to favoring the theory that scientific theories should be falsifiable, meaning if a hypothesis cannot create testable predictions, it is not considered science.

THEORY DEPENDENCE

Basic observations can be interpreted in different ways based on an individual's theories. For example, while it is common knowledge today that Earth rotates, earlier scientists believed the sun moved and Earth stayed still. Therefore, when an observation (which involves cognition and perception) is interpreted by a theory, it is referred to as theory-laden. According to philosopher and physicist Thomas Kuhn, it is impossible to isolate a hypothesis from the theory's influence (which is grounded in observation). Kuhn states that new paradigms (based on observations) are chosen when they do a better job than older paradigms in explaining scientific problems.

COHERENTISM

According to coherentism, theories and statements can be justified as the result of being a part of a coherent system. This system can pertain to the beliefs of a particular scientist or to the scientific community.

PSEUDOSCIENCE

Pseudoscience refers to those theories and doctrines that fail to follow the scientific method. Essentially, pseudoscience is nonscience that poses as science. While theories such as intelligent design, homeopathy, and astrology may serve other purposes, they cannot be considered a true type of science because they cannot be falsified and their methods conflict with results that are generally accepted. The disciplines used for investigating sciences simply cannot be applied to these types of theories. This is not to say that all nonscience is considered to be pseudoscience, however. Religion and metaphysics are two such examples of nonscientific phenomena.

BARUCH SPINOZA (1632–1677)

The naturalistic philosopher

Baruch Spinoza is considered one of the great rationalist philosophers of the seventeenth century. Spinoza was born on November 24, 1632, in Amsterdam's Portuguese-Jewish community. Spinoza was an incredibly gifted student, and it is believed that his congregation was grooming him to become a rabbi. When he was seventeen years old, however, Spinoza had to stop his studies to help run his family's business. On July 27, 1656, Spinoza was excommunicated from Amsterdam's Sephardic community for reasons still unknown (though it is believed that it was a response to Spinoza's emerging thoughts that would come to define his philosophy).

The philosophy of Baruch Spinoza was incredibly radical, and he had very naturalistic views on morality, God, and human beings. Spinoza denied that the soul is immortal and rejected the idea that God is providential. Instead, he argued that the Law was not given by God or binding on Jews any longer.

By 1661, Spinoza had lost all faith and religious commitment and no longer lived in Amsterdam. While living in Rijnsburg, he composed several treatises; however, only his 1663 exposition on Descartes's *Principles of Philosophy* would be published under his name during his lifetime. By 1663, Spinoza began to write his most profound philosophical text, *Ethics*; however, he stopped writing it to work on his controversial *Theological-Political Treatise*, which was published anonymously in 1670. The controversy surrounding *Theological-Political Treatise* made Spinoza abstain from publishing any more of his work, and in 1676, Spinoza met with Leibniz to discuss his recently completed *Ethics*, which he dared not publish. Upon his death in 1677, Spinoza's friends published his writing posthumously; however, his writing was banned throughout Holland.

SPINOZA'S *THEOLOGICAL-POLITICAL TREATISE*

In his most controversial work, *Theological-Political Treatise*, Baruch Spinoza attempted to show the truths behind religion and scripture, and undermine the political power that religious authorities held over the people.

Spinoza's View on Religion

Spinoza critiqued not only Judaism, but all organized religions, and claimed that philosophy must be separate from theology, especially with regard to reading scripture. The purpose of theology, according to Spinoza, is to maintain obedience, while the purpose of philosophy is to understand rational truth.

For Spinoza, "Love thy neighbor" is God's only message, and religion has turned into superstition, with words on a page meaning more than what the words represent. To Spinoza, the Bible was not a divine creation; rather, one should look at it like they would any other historical text, and because (he believed) it was written over many centuries, its content is unreliable. Miracles, according to Spinoza, do not exist and all have natural explanations; however, he claimed, people choose to not seek out such explanations. While Spinoza believed that prophesies did come from God, he claimed that they were not privileged knowledge.

Spinoza argued that in order to show God respect, the Bible needs to be re-examined in order to find a "true religion." He rejected the idea of "chosen-ness" found in Judaism, and argued that people are on the same level and that there should be one, national religion. Spinoza then revealed his political agenda and claimed that the ideal form of government is a democracy, because in a democracy there is the least abuse of power.

SPINOZA'S *ETHICS*

In his most extensive and significant work, *Ethics*, Baruch Spinoza takes on the traditional idea of God, religion, and human nature.

God and Nature

In his *Theological-Political Treatise*, Spinoza began to describe his beliefs that God is nature and that nature is God, and that it is incorrect to assume that God has human characteristics. In *Ethics*, Spinoza further expands upon his thoughts on God and nature. Everything that exists in the universe, according to Spinoza, is a part of nature (and therefore, God), and all things in nature follow identical basic laws. Spinoza takes a naturalistic approach (which was quite radical at the time) and claims that humans can be understood and explained in the same ways as anything else in nature, for humans are no different from the natural world.

Spinoza rejected the idea that God created the world out of nothing at a particular time. Instead, he claimed that our system of reality can be considered its own ground and that there is no supernatural element, just nature and God.

The Human

In the second part of *Ethics*, Spinoza focuses on the nature and origin of humans. Spinoza claimed that the two attributes of God that humans are aware of having are thought and extension. Modes of thought include ideas, while modes of extension include physical bodies, and the two act as separate essences. Bodily events are the results of a causal series of other bodily events and determined only by the laws that correspond to extension, while ideas are only the result of other ideas and follow their own set of laws. Therefore, there is not any type of causal interaction between the mental and the physical;

however, they are correlated and parallel to one another, so that with every mode of extension, there is a corresponding mode of thought.

Because thought and extension are attributes of God, they are two ways in which one can understand nature and God. Unlike Descartes's dualism, Spinoza's theory does not claim that there exist two separate substances. Rather, thought and extension are two expressions of one thing: a human.

Knowledge

Spinoza claimed that, like God, the mind of a human has ideas. These ideas, which are based on perceptual, sensory, and qualitative (like pain and pleasure) information, do not lead one to have true or adequate knowledge of the world because they are being perceived through the order of nature. This method of perception is a never-ending source of error and is referred to as "knowledge from random experience."

According to Spinoza, the second type of knowledge is reason. When one has an adequate idea, he attains it through a rational and orderly manner, and these ideas have a true understanding of a thing's essence. An adequate idea of something is able to grasp all of the causal connections and show that it is a certain way, why it is a certain way, and how it is a certain way. One can never have an adequate idea through sense experience alone.

Spinoza's notion of the adequate idea shows a great optimism in human capabilities unlike those seen before. According to Spinoza, humans have the capability to know all there is to know of nature and, therefore, know all there is to know of God.

Actions and Passions

Spinoza went to great lengths to prove that humans are a part of nature. By showing this, Spinoza implied that humans do not have freedom, for the mind and ideas are a result of a causal series of ideas that follow thought (which is an attribute from God), and actions are caused by natural events.

Spinoza then divides affects (emotions like anger, love, pride, envy, etc., which also follow nature) into passions and actions. When an event is caused as the result of our nature (like knowledge or adequate ideas), then the mind is acting. When an event within ourselves occurs as the result of something outside of our nature, then we are being acted upon and being passive. Regardless of whether we are acting or being acted upon, a change occurs within our mental or physical capacities. Spinoza claimed that all beings have an essence of striving to persevere, and that an affect is a change in this power.

According to Spinoza, humans should strive to free themselves of passions and become active. However, since being free of passions is not entirely possible, humans must try to restrain and moderate them. In becoming active and restraining passions, humans become "free" in the sense that whatever occurs will be the result of one's own nature, and not from external forces. This process will also free humans from the ups and downs of life. For Spinoza, humans need to free themselves from relying on imagination and the senses. Passions show how external things can affect our powers.

Virtue and Happiness

In *Ethics*, Spinoza argued that humans should control evaluations and attempt to minimize the influence of passions and external objects. This is done through virtue, which Spinoza describes as the pursuit and understanding of adequate ideas and knowledge. In the end, this means striving for knowledge of God (the third type of knowledge). Knowledge of God creates a love for objects that is not a passion, but blessedness. This is the understanding of the universe, as well as virtue and happiness.

PHILOSOPHY OF RELIGION

Understanding religion

The philosophical study of religion deals with the notions of miracles, prayer, the nature and existence of God, how religion and other value-systems relate to one another, and the problem of evil. The philosophy of religion is not theology, so it does not concern itself with the question of "What is God?" Rather, philosophy of religion looks at the themes and concepts found in religious traditions.

RELIGIOUS LANGUAGE

Religious language can often be viewed as mysterious, imprecise, and vague. In the twentieth century, philosophers began to challenge the standard religious language and attempted to reject any claims that were nonempirical, claiming them to be meaningless. This school of thought was known as logical positivism.

According to logical positivists, only those claims that contained empirical inferences or were from mathematics and logic could be deemed meaningful. This meant that many religious statements, even those that pertained to God (like "Yahweh is a compassionate and gracious God"), could not be verified and were therefore deemed meaningless.

In the second half of the twentieth century, as many philosophers began to find the claims of logical positivism to be problematic and the work in language by Ludwig Wittgenstein and the work in naturalism by Willard van Orman Quine became increasingly more popular, logical positivism began to wane. By the 1970s, the school of thought had practically collapsed, opening the door for new theories and interpretations of religious language.

After logical positivism, there were two schools of thought pertaining to religious language: realism and antirealism. Those who believed in realism believed that the language corresponds to what actually happened, while those who believed in antirealism believed that the language does not correspond to reality (rather, religious language refers to human behavior and experience).

THE PROBLEM OF EVIL

The most significant argument against theism is known as "the problem of evil." The problem of evil can be stated in many different ways:

The Logical Problem of Evil

First identified by Epicurus, the logical problem of evil is perhaps the strongest objection to the existence of God. According to Epicurus, there exist four possibilities:

1. If God wishes to prevent evil and is not able to, then God is feeble.
2. If God is able to get rid of evil but does not want to, then God is malevolent.
3. If God does not wish to get rid of evil and is not able to get rid of evil, then God is malevolent and feeble, and therefore, he is not God.
4. If God wants to get rid of evil and is able to get rid of evil, then why does evil exist in the world, and why has God not gotten rid of it?

St. Thomas Aquinas responded to the logical problem of evil by stating that it is not clear whether or not the absence of evil would make the world a better place, for without evil, there would be no meaning to kindness, justice, fairness, or self-sacrifice. Another argument against the logical problem of evil, known as the "unknown purpose defense," states that since God can never be truly known, humans have limitations when trying to guess God's motivations.

The Empirical Problem of Evil

Created by David Hume, the empirical problem of evil claims that if one were not exposed to prior commitments such as religious convictions, the experience of evil in the world would lead one to atheism and the notion of a God that is good and omnipotent could not exist.

The Probabilistic Argument from Evil

This is the argument that the very existence of evil is proof that there is no God.

THEODICY

Theodicy is a branch of philosophy that tries to reconcile the belief in a God that is benevolent, omniscient, and omnipotent with the existence of evil and suffering. Theodicy accepts that God is able to end evil and that evil exists, and tries to understand why God has not stopped it. One of the most well-known theodicy theories is Leibniz's claim that this world is the most optimal among other possible worlds and that because it was created by a God that is perfect, it must be the most balanced and best possible world there can be.

ARGUMENTS FOR
THE EXISTENCE OF GOD

There are three main types of arguments for the existence of God: ontological, cosmological, and teleological.

Ontological Arguments

Ontological arguments use *a priori* abstract reasoning to claim that the concept of God and the ability to speak of God implies that God must exist. When we speak about God, we are talking about a perfect being; nothing is greater. Since we would be better having a God that exists rather than a God that doesn't and we refer to God as a perfect being, we imply that God exists.

Ontological arguments are flawed, for they can be used to show the existence of any perfect thing. According to Kant, existence is a property of concepts and not of objects.

The Cosmological Argument

The cosmological argument claims that since the world and universe exist, this implies that they were brought into existence, and are kept in existence, by a being. There must be a "first mover," which is God, because an infinite regress is simply not possible. There are two types of cosmological arguments:

1. Modal (which states that the universe might not have existed and therefore there needs to be an explanation for why it does)
2. Temporal (which states that there must have been a point in time when the universe began to exist, and this existence must have been caused by something outside of the universe, which is God)

The Teleological Argument

The teleological argument, which is also referred to as intelligent design, claims that because there is order in the world and universe, the world must have been created by a being that had the specific purpose of creating life in mind.

MIRACLES

In philosophy of religion, there is much debate over what can and cannot be considered a miracle. When discussing miracles, philosophers refer to events that are unusual and cannot be explained through natural causes. These events, according to some philosophers, must therefore be the result of a divinity.

David Hume objected to the notion of miracles, calling them a "violation to the laws of nature." Hume argued that the only evidence to support miracles is witness testimony, while evidence to support the laws of nature is acquired through the uniform experience of people over time. Therefore, a miracle's witness testimony needs to be greater than the support for the laws of nature, and since there is not sufficient evidence to show this, it is unreasonable to believe that these types of violations to the laws of nature can occur.

Others have objected to Hume's take on miracles, however, believing them not to be violations to the laws of nature. These philosophers argue that the laws of nature describe what is likely to occur under specific conditions, and therefore, miracles are just exceptions to the usual processes. Philosophers of religion argue that Hume has an inadequate understanding of probability and that looking at the frequency of an event occurring is not enough to determine probability.

Index